My Yesterday Could Be Your Today

GREG CARTER

A survivor's story of his battle and victory over cancer

Scripture taken from *The Amplified New Testament*

ISBN 0-939241-98-6

Copyright © 2001 Greg Carter

Greg Carter
8530 South Harrison Park Rd.
Laconia, IN 47135
812-969-2721

Printed in the United States of America

Acknowledgments

Let me take a moment to acknowledge those who helped me overcome:

My wife Ronda, who like a rock, became a tremendous source of stability during journey.

My parents, Ned and Bonnie Carter, who unflinchingly believed God for my healing.

My sister, Marcia Brown, who constantly encouraged me in phone conversations peppered with medical advice.

The church at Grace Tabernacle, who loved me more than they loved themselves, giving up chunks of their personal time to constantly pray for my healing.

The churches and pastors of Southern Harrison County for their special prayer sessions.

Kevin Helton for cover design.

Sandi Pike for editing and correcting my manuscript.

Foreword

"You have cancer!" Words that strike fear through the heart of hundreds of people everyday. In many cases, cancer is a death sentence and when the diagnosis is made you may feel as if you are being suddenly and unexpectedly sentenced to death row for something you never did. When a person has cancer, even though they are alive, death begins to take over their body. This is a story of a man who fought back from the brink of death all the way to a clean bill of health by the power of the word of God.

Pastor Greg Carter was diagnosed with bladder cancer in 1995. I have known Pastor Greg and his wife, Ronda, for fourteen years. Theirs was the first church I had the privilege of ministering in on my very first ministry trip to the U.S.A. in 1987. At that time, the town of Laconia, Indiana, had a population of 65, but the Carter's church overflowed with people during my last crusade there. Their church is a lighthouse to the whole community. Pastors Greg and Ronda have been so faithful, serving God all these years in Laconia, and it was a shock to me to hear that he had been diagnosed with cancer.

Even though the word "cancer" strikes fear in the heart of most people, Greg was determined not to give up and just lay down and die, but to fight it. During this dark time, he came and joined us in several of our revival meetings, that we were conducting all over the nation, and we would pray with him, lay our hands on him and trust God with him for his miracle. We felt that God would touch his body if we could just get him saturated under the anointing of the Holy Spirit.

We need each other. We need to stand with our heavenly family. We are the body of Christ. We need to be strong for our sisters and brothers when they are under attack. We need to pray for each other and join our faith together with theirs. We need to press in with them for their miracle.

Pastor Greg Carter put his trust in God and His word and he has come through this battle victoriously. Thanks to the power of God, now five years later he has a clean bill of health. Once again, we can rejoice in the fact that God is faithful! Even cancer must bow its knee to the King of kings and the Lord of lords!

I believe that this book will be a great blessing and an inspiration to you.

        Dr. Rodney M. Howard-Browne
        Tampa, Florida
        July 2001

Contents

Introduction
You Need to Hear a Survivor's Story ix

Chapter 1
All is Well, Then Suddenly 1

Chapter 2
Difficult Decisions 21

Chapter 3
Confronting My Situation 31

Chapter 4
Daily Living According to Scripture 47

Chapter 5
Controlling Your Mind 55

Chapter 6
There is Hope Again 67

Chapter 7
Finding a Relationship with God in
the Midst of Your Problem 75

Chapter 8
  Conforming Me to His Image 85

Introduction

This is not a "How To" book or a book about my great overcoming faith. It is simply the story of an 18-month chapter of my life. In January 1996 because of bladder cancer, I was given less than a year to live. I became all too familiar with the place of residence called *the Valley of the Shadow of Death.*

This book details my journey *through* the most difficult time of my life. *Through* is a marvelous word. Though I descended into the valley of shadow of death, I did not stay there but passed through. To this day when I hear the expression, "I'm sorry you have to go through this," it brings a smile to my face because if I have to make an appearance in a difficult spot, I want to go through it and not remain there.

In the following pages, I want to encourage those going through a devastating time on their journey through life. All the answers to your questions are not here, but hopefully, enough answers to encourage you through your trial. I have tried to share honestly my ups and downs, my highs and lows, and my times of great faith and my times of utter despair. I did not win all the battles, but eventually, I won the war.

When I was struggling to keep afloat, I often read accounts of those who had lived to tell about the same battle I was waging. Those who have engaged in a battle for their life and lived to tell about it have much to say to those presently in the fight. Sometimes you need to hear a survivor's story. It is my prayer that this book will be a lifeline thrown out in a sea of turmoil. May God Almighty encourage you in His grace as you read this book.

CHAPTER 1

All is Well, Then Suddenly

Life is what happens while we are making other plans. Not realizing that devastating events lurked just around the corner, my future with all my carefully laid plans was about to be drastically altered. The Holy Scriptures tell us to take no thought for tomorrow because each day has enough trouble of its own (Matthew 13:11). But even as a minister full of life, trying to live in the flow of God, I, like so many others, lived my life with all sorts of future plans laid out thinking that nothing was going to stop their fulfillment.

Before a scheduled mission trip to India in October, Steve Rayborn, one of my closest friends and his wife Cindy were vacationing with Ronda and me in the Smokies in August of 1995. Steve and I love to play golf while our wives love to hit the outlet malls.

As I hit my tee shot on the first hole, I felt a twinge of pain that was unlike anything I had ever felt before. It was not severe, just strange, one that I could not put my finger on its source. As mysteriously as it came, it left and I felt no more sensations of pain on the front nine. At the turn while going to the bathroom, I noticed blood in my urine. I was no medical expert, but I knew enough that I needed to get it checked out as soon as possible.

Not wanting to ruin Ronda's vacation, I determined to tell her nothing. We would enjoy our week together and I would make an appointment with an urologist as soon as we got home. *Whatever is wrong is something simple, like an infection or non-malignant growth that will be easily treatable,* I assured myself each time I passed blood that week in Gatlinburg, TN. *I'll see a doctor, get some antibiotics, get over this thing and go on with my life.*

When we arrived home from vacation, I broke the news to Ronda and made an appointment with Dr. Joseph Bruckman at Southern Indiana Urology for the last Tuesday in August 1995. After an examination and urine analysis, Dr. Bruckman very compassionately informed me that there were cancer cells in my urine, and he needed to examine inside my urinary tract with a cystoscope. He scheduled the procedure for the following Monday.

Early Monday morning Ronda and I arrived at Floyd Memorial Hospital in New Albany, Indiana, and I was admitted as an outpatient. Dr. Bruckman performed a procedure inserting a cystoscope device into my urinary tract while I was under anesthesia. After completing the procedure, Dr. Bruckman signed release papers and scheduled an appointment on Thursday to discuss the results of the test. Ronda and I went home that afternoon fully assured that whatever the results would be, they would be something simple, treatable, and well within our limits to handle.

During the Wednesday evening service, many dear church friends prayed passionately for Ronda and I. We had a wonderful service and even with the next day's

The Lord is my shepherd; I shall not want. He maketh me to lie down in green pastures; He leadeth me beside the still waters. He restoreth my soul; He leadeth me in the paths of righteousness for His name's sake.

Yea, though I walk through the valley of the shadow of death, I will fear no evil; for Thou art with me; Thy rod and Thy staff they comfort me. Thou preparest a table before me in the presence of mine enemies; Thou anointest my head with oil; my cup runneth over.

Surely goodness and mercy shall follow me all the days of my life; and I will dwell in the house of the Lord for ever.

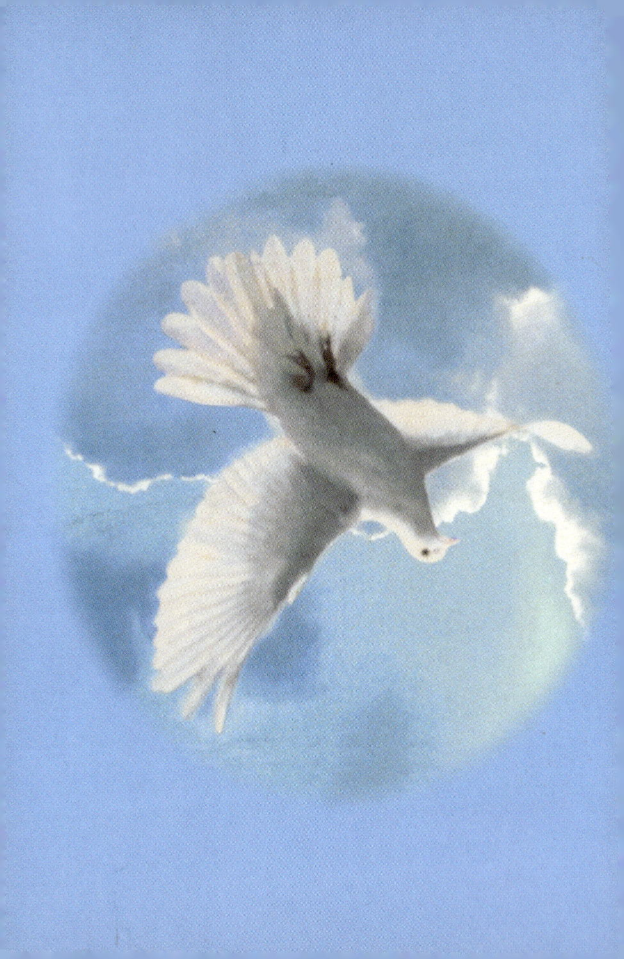

visit to the doctor, I felt a remarkable peace about my circumstances. Little did I know that in just a few short hours that peace would be shattered, and I would be embarking on a journey through the deepest wilderness I had ever known.

Some Kind of a Bad Dream

Thursday upon arriving at Dr. Bruckman's office and going through the routine preliminaries, I settled down in a soft chair and waited for my name to be called playing over and over in my mind all the possibilities of different diagnoses.

When my name was called, I took Ronda's hand and walked back through the corridor to the doctor's office. A nurse seated us and told us that the doctor would see us momentarily.

As Dr. Bruckman entered and sat across from us at his desk, I saw a look of deep concern and impending bad news in his countenance. Instead of any formalities of greeting, he simply began to read the biopsy report and his diagnosis based on the pathologist's findings.

His news—I had two malignant tumors Grade III Transitional Cell Carcinoma that had penetrated the wall of my bladder. The invasive cancer had penetrated so deeply that removing it through a cystoscope was not possible.

A radical cystecomy, a surgical procedure that involves removal of the bladder and the prostate gland, was the doctor's advised treatment. A urinary diversion known as an ileal loop would take the place of my cancerous bladder. A section of my colon would be used internally to direct the urine flow to an ostomy, or hole in my side that would drain into an appliance, literally a plastic bag attached to my abdomen. This device would require draining every few hours. I was assured that even with this inconvenience, I could return to a normal life.

"Today is Thursday and I would like to operate on Monday," were the words that I heard the doctor say, but they sounded as if they were coming from some distant place.

Both Ronda and I were completely stunned by the diagnosis. Never did we believe that anything of this magnitude could happen to me. I was a pastor, full of faith, preaching the Gospel, and praying for the sick at almost every church service. *This had to be some kind of bad dream.*

Mustering all the strength and courage I could, I asked Dr. Bruckman, "What if I choose to do nothing?"

He responded simply, "If you do not have your bladder removed, the cancer will penetrate through your bladder wall, spread to other areas, and you will die. Your only hope of long term survival is to have surgery."

After hearing this devastating news, I was in no shape to make any immediate decision about surgery. I asked for the weekend to think over the matter and pray for God's direction before I made any decision. Dr. Bruckman graciously consented, shook my hand, and scheduled an appointment for the following Monday.

The ride home was uncharacteristically quiet. Ronda and I could not even put into words the utter despair and helplessness we both felt. She drove weeping quietly as I stared at the familiar scenery along Highway 11, trying desperately to put a positive spin on my circumstances.

Sleep that night evaded us. Weeping softly, Ronda lay next to me while I battled spirits of fear and self-pity. I had handled some difficult situations before, but nothing like this. Doubts about the integrity of the God I served and my relationship to him began gnawing at my faith. *Why has God allowed this to happen to me?* and *Is there a way out?* were questions I had at that moment with no answers.

Friday morning, I became aware of the stark reality that it is hard to pray with faith when you are faced with a devastating medical report. I soon realized that my relationship with Jesus was going to have to expand to places that, spiritually, I had never been.

In a small community bad news travels fast and that evening at Grace Tabernacle's Friday evening intercessory prayer service, folks that did not normally participate came in force, to pray for my situation. If intensity of prayer and tears will get you healed, the cancer in my body did not stand a chance. I was amazed at the people that were standing with me touched with the feelings of my infirmity.

Waiting Upon God

Late Sunday evening I arrived at a course of action. After three days of prayer, a consultation with my sister, Marcia Brown, a registered nurse, and the consent of my wife, I decided to persuade Dr. Bruckman to give me some time to seek God for a healing. I understood the medical ramifications of such a decision, but I could not bring myself just to lie down and have surgery until I had given the Lord time to heal my body.

Our Monday morning consultation with the doctor went even better than I anticipated. Dr. Bruckman, a respected urologist, does things by the medical book, but he understood that as a pastor I was not going to have surgery until I had determined I had exhausted every spiritual avenue of healing.

Very reluctantly, making sure I completely understood the dangers of waiting, and with my full consent, Dr. Bruckman proposed we wait 90 days. After that period of time, I would have a second biopsy and if nothing had changed, I would consent to surgery. I left his office full of hope. *Surely,* I reasoned, *if God created the world in six days, taking care of my little problem in 90 days was nothing for Him.*

In the following three-month time frame, I engaged in some of the most intense times of spiritual warfare I had ever known. Daily, I prayed with intense fervor, seeking God's healing touch. I quoted the Word to myself to build my faith, submitted myself to all who wanted to pray for me, and underwent a personal inspection of my spiritual life to remove any defilement that might block a touch of God. I took several personal retreats to isolated places to spend large amounts of undisturbed time to seek God. My parents, Ned and Bonnie Carter accompanied Ronda and I to Brownsville Assembly of God in Pensacola, Florida hoping that God's healing power would touch me as He was touching others daily in the revival services. I did everything I could think of to stay in a spiritual atmosphere where God could find me and touch me.

Spiritual Journeys Can Have Unexpected Turns

Even though my physical symptoms were screaming otherwise, I arrived at the hospital for my December 4th cystoscope procedure charged with faith and confidence that the biopsy report would reveal God had touched me and that surgery would no longer be necessary.

Cystourethroscopy usually lasts a relative short time, and after a few hours in the recovery room and a glass of orange juice, the patient is sent home. This time I was not so fortunate. The scope had irritated my urinary tract and the opening to my bladder making urination difficult, and it was decided that I was to be kept overnight for observation.

Pain and discomfort can be detrimental to faith. After a very uncomfortable night, my spiritual disposition had shifted from anticipation of a good report to a horrible dread of a bad one. But as negative as my disposition was, it was about to take a nosedive.

The biopsy report revealed that not only did I still have Grade III Transitional Cell Carcinoma, but also it revealed that the tumors had increased in size and had invaded deeper into the wall of my bladder. Anger swept over me like a raging river. As Dr. Bruckman left the room, I asked everyone present to leave and give me some time. When the door to my room closed, and I was completely alone, I exploded. I threw pillows, urinals, pitchers, newspapers and magazines, anything that was not nailed down.

In my confusion, I had questions that demanded answers. Why hadn't God touched me? How, after such an intense time of spiritual warfare, could the situation grow worse? I was so angry with God for letting me down. I thought, *I could have been out robbing banks and committing adultery for the past 90 days and got this report.*

I sat down on the bed and looked upward, beholding only ceiling tile, and told the Lord that I would never preach another sermon, and just as soon as possible, I was going to resign my church, quit the ministry, and go back to teaching school. "It's your fault!" I shouted at God. "I have proclaimed to everyone that would listen that You were going to heal me and You didn't. How can I ever stand behind a pulpit again and proclaim anything good about You when You didn't hold up your end of the bargain?"

If there was ever an outburst that deserved a lightening bolt, that was it. But as my anger began to subside, I became fully aware that I could not become separated from God, the source of my help. I asked God's forgiveness for my outburst and direction for the decisions I would be forced to make in the coming days.

Hospitals are not conducive to the spiritual decision making process. According to the medical report if I wanted to be around much longer, I was going to have to undergo radical cystectomy, a surgical procedure that involved the removal of the bladder and prostate, requiring the wearing of a urostomy pouch, as well as, leaving me sexually dysfunctional.

Things were certainly not following the script I had written in my mind. My well thought out plans were that God would heal me in that 90-day period, we would have a celebration at church, God would get the glory, and I would go back to business as usual. Instead, I was facing a horrific surgery, a long recuperation, and spiritual egg on my face.

Thoughts, Plans, and Medical Options

I determined that if I was going to have medical intervention, I would become as informed as I could about all the possible avenues of treatment. The probability of wearing a urostomy pouch and being sexually dysfunctional at the age of 43 was a tough thing to swallow. The thought, *Some where, there is a doctor who has a more appealing option,* dominated my thinking for days.

Finally, the first ray of hope surfaced one Wednesday night before church as Paula Murphy, our dear friend, brought us some information she had gleaned from the Internet. She brought us several pages of medical reports about a procedure call Neo-bladder. Neo-bladder surgery involved the construction of a continent urinary reservoir from a section of the patient's colon. A nerve sparing procedure, in some cases, could also be performed, restoring sexual function. Of all the options I had information on, this certainly seemed to be the one I was more attracted to, and the medical center where the procedure was performed was only 125 miles from my home.

At our next consultation with Dr. Bruckman, I expressed my desire not to have the ileal loop procedure and wanted to check into the Neo-bladder. He graciously agreed to contact Dr. Randall Rowland at the IUPUI Medical Center, one of the few places this procedure is done, in Indianapolis, Indiana.

After Dr. Bruckman's call, Dr. Rowland, head of Urology at IUPUI, agreed to meet with me on and discuss the possibility of surgery. Although, no where near elation, I was slowly coming to grips with the reality that I was going to have to make the best of a bad situation.

Ronda and I found Dr. Rowland, a world-renowned surgeon, to be very kind and compassionate. After reviewing Dr. Bruckman's findings and going over the results of the most recent CT scan, Dr. Rowland agreed to take my case and scheduled me for surgery three weeks later. I took a degree of comfort in his knowledge and experience. His vast medical expertise included over 300 of these procedures. If I had to have this surgery, this gentleman was certainly the man I wanted doing it.

Urination was becoming increasingly more difficult and frequent. I also felt like a spiritual failure to a degree because my faith could not overcome this illness that was waging war in my physical body. It all seemed, at times, like a bad dream that would not go away. To make matters worse, I felt shunned by some of my Christian friends because I had agreed to surgery, and to them, I was not taking a stand of faith.

I knew in my spirit that the next three weeks, prior to surgery, would be a wild roller coaster ride of emotions, accentuated by both highs and lows. My hope was that I could ride this thing out while I continued to minister to the needs of my congregation.

God always has a way of escape (see 1 Corinthians 10:13), no matter how difficult the trial and that escape is usually spiritual growth. The fiery ordeals that all of us encounter sometime in life will either make us or break us. If we determine to pass through whatever spiritual wilderness we find ourselves in, it will require us to develop spiritual strength we did not possess when we began the journey. In the middle of the trek, we run out of vitality and if we are to survive, we must allow the Holy Spirit to develop within us spiritual resources that were there all along, just unknown to us.

Encouragement Knows No Distance

Encouragement came to me from a phone call from Rodney Howard-Browne, a well-known evangelist from South Africa. When Rodney arrived in the United States in 1987, the first church he ministered in was the church I pastor, Grace Tabernacle, Laconia, IN. During that time, I was hosting a weekly television program, *Still in the Spirit,* and Rodney did a month long series of programs with me sharing his vision for America.

Over the next few years, Rodney conducted several revival meetings in our church, and we developed a bond of friendship. After his last visit to our church in 1991, I had little contact with Rodney because the scope of his international ministry had broadened well beyond the little town of Laconia, IN, and I was thrilled that he was being used so mightily by God.

My 15-year old son, Dane, desperately wanting to see me healed, called Rodney and asked him to pray for me. Rodney, however, did more than just pray. At his expense, the week before my surgery, he invited Ronda and me to attend his Winter Camp Meeting in Tampa. Hotel accommodations, meals and transportation, as well as, spiritual refreshing were waiting for us as we landed at the Tampa International Airport.

Bad weather conditions delayed our flight out of Louisville, KY causing us to miss the Monday morning service and part of the evening one. A representative of Rodney's ministry met us at the airport and whisked us to the Tampa Sun Dome where thousands of hungry believers from all parts of the globe soaked in the presence of God

By the time we entered the building, the worship service was just coming to its conclusion. Trying to be as inconspicuous as possible, Ronda and I slipped into our seats, removed our jackets, and tried to take in one of the most spiritual atmospheres we had ever been in. Thousands of people were worshipping the Lord and the presence of God was so thick you could cut it with a knife. *Surely,* I thought, *There is healing in this place.*

In the midst of this glorious atmosphere, I heard my name being called out. Rodney had spotted us and wanted me to come to the platform for prayer. As I walked down the aisle, Rodney told the audience who I was and why I was there. I heard him say that he was going to pray for me in every service and believe God for a miracle. Those were the last words I heard.

As Rodney stretched his hand toward me, the power of God hit me with such force I fell to the floor. I felt as if I was plugged into an electric outlet. Rodney literally lay on top of me much like Elisha did the Shummanite's widow's son, tearfully asking God to heal my body. For the next three hours, I experienced the most profound touch of God I had ever had upon my life. Wave after wave of the power of God rushed through my body causing my whole body to vibrate and tremble.

When the spiritual fog began to subside, I lifted my hands toward heaven and began to implore the Lord to heal my body. After an experience like that, I reasoned that surely the next item on the Lord's agenda would be to sweep over my body and cleanse me from sickness. Between sobs I prayed, "Heal me Jesus." "Heal me Jesus."

The Holy Spirit spoke to me as clearly as I had ever heard Him speak in my life, "Greg, there are things in your life that concern Me much more than cancer." The Holy Spirit began to reveal to me conditions of my heart; the pride, the stubbornness, and the rebellion that existed that were hindering me more than any physical infirmity. Though I could sense nothing happening in the physical realm, I could sense that God was performing spiritual surgery, opening up areas in my life that were under a facade of denial. In the eyes of God, the condition of the heart always takes precedence over the physical condition.

The rest of the week in Tampa was a wonderful time of rest and relaxation. Rodney's ministry team treated us like royalty. The services blessed both Ronda and me, and though my physical condition was continuing to deteriorate, I sensed that God had done something marvelous in me. I had gone to the conference with the express desire of getting rid of the cancer, but instead, I left with a deep sense that God was going to do a marvelous work in my spirit. And I knew my fighting a physical infirmity was going to be the avenue He was going to use to accomplish that work.

Back Home Again in Indiana

Immediately after arriving back in Indiana, I began to prepare myself mentally for surgery. The radical cystectomy and the neo-bladder surgery was a complicated medical procedure averaging 9 to 11 hours on the operating table accompanied by a 7 to 10 day stay in the hospital. After the surgery and release from the hospital, a six-week recuperation process is required for healing and personal training for the new process of urination that the neo-bladder requires. I don't care how close you walked to God getting prepared for all that stretched my spirituality awfully thin.

My surgery was scheduled for 6:30 a.m. Monday morning, and I elected not to spend Sunday night in the hospital but to drive the 125 miles to Indianapolis the morning of the surgery. I wanted to be able to attend both services at church and give the Lord one last opportunity to spare me all the trouble and medical expense. Services were wonderful that last Sunday, but no miracle. I was headed for surgery.

That night prior to surgery was a sleepless one. An upset stomach caused by the last round of antibiotics, an awful sense of dread of surgery, and anxiety made rest impossible. By 3:30 a.m. we were on Interstate 65 headed for the IUPUI Medical Center in Indianapolis. Ronda had driven this stretch of road hundreds of times before, but this trip was one for the memory books. Our conversation was limited as we both fought to maintain faith and a positive attitude that God was somehow going to work all this out for our good and His glory (see Romans 8:28).

Preparation for surgery was a whirlwind of activity. The last few minutes prior to my walk to the operating room were filled with consent forms being signed, IV lines being inserted, and prayer and encouragement from my family. One last time, the medical staff went over the procedure with me. I was going to have a cystectomy with continent urinary reservoir construction, a procedure where the bladder and the prostate gland are removed and a bladder is constructed from a section of the colon. I would be in surgery 8-10 hours, followed by 24 hours in Intensive Care, and if all went well, taken to a regular room to recuperate for 10 days.

As a precaution, they measured me for an ileal loop, a more standard urinary diversion that consists of a stoma that drains into an external bag. The ileal loop would be used only if the cancer was in areas that the CT scan had not revealed. I so distinctly remember looking at the clock in the operating room. It read, 6:50 a.m. and I made a mental note that the next time I would open my eyes, it would be somewhere around 5:00 p.m. The last thing I remember prior to falling asleep was asking the presence of the Holy Spirit to surround me in the operating room.

My Definition of "Bad" Was About to be Revised

In what seemed like but a moment of time, I could hear my name being called out. The sounds were coming from a fog that was so thick I could not see who was speaking or why they wanted me. As I struggled to respond, my eyes searched for the clock on the wall. It was 11:00 a.m. and my hand instinctively reached for my right side and felt the urostomy pouch in place. I was in a deep fog, but I had enough wits about me to realize that something had gone wrong during the surgery.

Nausea produced by the fear of the unknown swept over me like a river. I desperately needed two things:

something to relieve the sickness in my stomach, and someone to tell me what went wrong in surgery. An antinausea medicine took care of the first need and the appearance of my wife took care of the second.

Ronda has always been a fortress of strength, and rarely, in our 24 years of marriage had I ever seen her shaken. As she held my hand and began to speak, I could feel the tremors that ran through her body. Very briefly and concisely she gave me the surgeon's report. The surgical procedure had been abandoned because of the discovery of grossly positive lymph nodes. I had been given an ileal loop, the very procedure I had gone to IUPUI to avoid. According to Dr. Rowland's vast experience, he estimated that I had six months to a year to live.

The suddenness and intensity of the news so completely stunned me that I did not know how to react. It is amazing the things that cross your mind when confronted with such devastating news. I thought that evidently God was through with me and I would have only a limited time to close the book on my earthly existence, and I was glad my life insurance policy would take care of Ronda and the kids.

The rest of that Monday was a haze of voices talking around me. I vaguely remember the steady stream of family and friends, who after hearing the news, had either visited to pray for me or to comfort Ronda. I remember thinking, *This is like lying in the funeral home and seeing and hearing people talking to you and about you, but not having the ability to participate in the conversation.* I longed for a clear mind and for the effects of the powerful drugs from the surgery to subside.

What am I going to do? How am I going to handle all this? Am I really going to die?

Tuesday morning dawned and finally, the fog in my brain lifted. I could think clearly, but my reality had not changed. The cancer in my bladder had found its way into my lymphatic system, and the doctors were certain that it would only be a matter of time before it would invade my liver and lungs. I had a sixteen-inch vertical incision in my abdomen, a gastric tube down my throat, a urostomy pouch on my side, and a prognosis of my 44th birthday being my last.

The surgeon and the oncologists were to visit, and I had a list of questions to ask them. Everything I had heard had been second-hand information, and I was anxiously awaiting their visit so I could hear their prognosis first-hand. Ten minutes before their 10:00 visit, the phone rang.

Steve Marcum, Reluctant Prophet

As I answered the call, the voice on the other end was sobbing so hard that I could not recognize the voice. The man simply kept saying, "This is Steve." I have several close friends and cousins named Steve, but finally recognized Steve as Steve Marcum, pastor of Graceland Baptist Church in New Albany, Indiana.

Steve began to shout to me, "You are not going to die! You are not going to die! It does not matter what the doctors tell you. You are not going to die!" Through his sobbing he explained that I was not even on his mind as he was reading his daily devotional which happened to be the story of Hezekiah found in 2 Kings 20 in which Hezekiah had a sickness unto death, but the Lord relented and gave Hezekiah more time.

Steve explained to me that the Holy Spirit had come upon him so strongly that he had to call and tell me that the Lord had spoken to his heart that I was going to live and not die. Our conversation was short but encouraging. Of the thousands of phone conversations I have had in my lifetime, that one call was the most unique and uplifting I had ever received.

The Holy Spirit could not have chosen an instrument that would validate His word to me more than Steve Marcum could. Steve comes from a solid and conservative Southern Baptist background and has never been give to emotional hype. If the messenger had been one of my Pentecostal buddies, I would have been concerned that they were speaking a message to me birthed more out of their desire for me to make it rather than being a spokesman for the Holy Spirit.

My conservation with Steve was the first spark of life I had felt for the past 24 hours. The timing of the message took on tremendous significance because no sooner than my conversation ended with Steve, Dr. Rowland making his morning rounds walked into my room with a somewhat somber appearance.

Which Report to Believe?

Dr. Rowland explained to me that he had abandoned the radical cystecomy procedure because of the appearance of cancer in my lymphatic system. He had removed 18 cancerous lymph nodes and diverted my urinary tract through an ileal loop because the tumors in my bladder were close to shutting down the normal urinary function.

Dr. Rowland is a very compassionate man and I could tell that he preferred not to have much influence on my decision making process. But I had to make some big decisions about future treatment, and I needed his expert medical advice. I pressed him as hard as I could to squeeze from him every detail about his view of my medical condition. From his involvement with many others that had the degree of lymphatic involvement I had, these realities surfaced: He had never had a patient with my current medical condition live any longer than 11 months, and I could have as little as two months or as much as six months to a year according to how fast the cancer spread.

When I pressed Dr. Rowland as to what he would do if he was in my condition based on his dealings with the same scenario in others, he simply told me that he would not take the chemotherapy, "But go home, get my house in order, and enjoy what remaining time I had left." He patted my hand and left Ronda and me to mull over the devastating prognosis.

In a matter of an hour, I had had two very contrasting reports. One report was that I was going to live, and the other report was that I was going to be dead within a year. Both reports were floating around in my mind as two oncologists from the hospital visited to give me information on what type of treatments were available. Their faces looked like talking heads as they explained to me that standard treatment for my degree of cancer was not very promising. Only about 20% of patients had any response at all, and the greatest benefit from the treatment they offered was that it would simply delay the inevitable and buy me a little more time.

As they talked to me, my thoughts drifted to the images of people I had pastored that had suffered the devastating side effects of chemotherapy. The treatment had left them unable to enjoy any quality of life. I had seen enough of it that I had made up my mind a long time ago that if faced with terminal cancer, chemotherapy would not be an option for me. I thanked the doctors for their time and told them that after I was home and able to think clearly, I would contact their office and inform them of my decision.

No Matter How Dark, Light Penetrates

Ronda and I determined that we would make the best of my 10-day hospital stay, remain as positive as possible, and not make any decisions until we got home. I needed the atmosphere of my church and friends and needed to hear the clear voice of the Holy Spirit.

My ten-day stay at IUPUI Medical Center included my 44th birthday. Even though being 130 miles from home, over fifty friends and family members visited that day loaded with gifts and cards. I was blessed that day with a tremendous outpouring of love that made me all the more anxious to get home and back to church that I pastored.

In spite of all the negatives going on in my life, the church I had pastored for 17 years was having a real move of God. Since the day of my diagnosis, people had met every night at the church to pray for me and seek God's guidance for the future. As they united together to wage war for my life, the Holy Spirit fell in such a powerful way that it swept out all negativity, doubt, and fear.

These precious friends of mine determined that they were going to grab hold of the altar and not let go until my recovery was certain, and in the process, spiritual renewal began to move in the body of the church having a profound effect on everyone attending those nightly sessions. There was no doom and gloom at Grace Tabernacle but a strong expectancy that I was going to get a miracle.

During my stay in the hospital, call after call encouraged me not to lose hope and faith but to press into God and expect His intervention in my situation. Even with all the outward circumstances going on in my life, these calls of encouragement kept the despair from overtaking me. It seemed as if each call was perfectly timed to meet whatever mental battle I was having.

The remainder of my hospital stay was devoted to learning how to deal with a urostomy and all the care necessary to keep it functional. Wearing a bag was going to bring about some major adjustments in my lifestyle. Flanges, snap-on bags, and baggy clothes would become a part of my daily existence. In the midst of these personal profound life adjustments, I was beginning to see that the Lord was taking me down a road that was going to rearrange my entire perspective on life.

The day of my dismissal was dark, dreary and snowy, but my spirits were soaring as we drove away from the hospital. I was on my way home where I could control my environment, could seek God without interruption, and could be surrounded by family and friends. As we turned off State Highway 11 onto South Harrison Park Road toward the church a banner caught my attention, *Welcome Home Greg and Ronda.*

Tears begin to fill my eyes as I looked down the entire 1/4 mile stretch between the highway and the church as sign after sign proclaimed not only the church's compassion for us, but also signs that proclaimed the healing power of the God we serve. I was absolutely overwhelmed with emotion.

CHAPTER 2

Difficult Decisions

Overwhelmed is an inadequate adjective to describe the rush of emotions that engulfed me as Ronda and I drove the short distance from Highway 11 to South Harrison Park Road to the church. The ill effects of a 12-day stay in the hospital seemed to vanish, as I read banner after banner proclaiming God's love and concern for my situation.

It was after 9:00 p.m. on a Tuesday evening, yet the parking lot at the church was full of cars. I convinced Ronda to stop, but only after promising we would just sneak in the back door, go upstairs, and look into the sanctuary from the sound room.

As we walked in the back door, I could hear the cries of intercession and shouts of praise flowing from the sanctuary. The intensity of their prayers completely overruled any thoughts of negativity and defeat. Those dear saints prayed fervently for my complete victory. From no closer than the hallway, I felt a charge of spiritual renewal that energized my faith.

Nothing could have kept me from joining in with what was happening in the sanctuary that night. Tears blinded me as I joined my spirit with those who interceded for me. In my entire Christian experience, that memory is forever etched as the time I felt more love from family, friends, and the Lord than I had ever known.

For twelve days I had been bombarded by bad news. I had had little time to pray, read the Word, or get any kind of direction from God, yet God's power and presence was like a sweet stream of refreshing. I began to pray for others and saw God's presence and anointing flow through me even though I had been out of spiritual commission lying in a hospital bed. My faith began to soar and the thought, *Maybe God's not through with me,* began dancing around in my mind.

Hope is a precious commodity, and our faith brings us the things we hope for. Hope is future, but faith is now. Hope for my future, which had been in short supply, began to flow into the reservoir of my spirit. Suddenly, to a man who thought that he might not have a future sprang the possibility "...with God, all things are possible" (see Mark 10:27).

As I looked over those gathered in the sanctuary that night, I was amazed that on a snowy Tuesday evening so many had ventured out to pray for me. Life, for all of us has many demands pulling at us and most folks never lack for something to do. I kept thinking, *Why have these people given up what they wanted to do, to do something for me?*

The answer came as I looked into the eyes of several saints in a prayer circle. I realized that during that season in their lives, they loved me more than they loved themselves. What a powerful revelation that just as Jesus loved us more than He loved himself, so the Church was loving me and putting me ahead of their own agenda.

There is power in our lives only to the degree that we are willing to give it up. If we want to find our lives, we must lose them (see Matt. 16:25). God's power and presence is manifested when people put other's needs ahead of their own. If we love others more than ourselves, we are displaying the form of love that motivated Jesus to be nailed to a cross.

God moved mightily through the obedience of Jesus Christ. Jesus could have come down from the cross any time He wanted, but His loving others more than himself produced a moving of the hand of God that resulted in the salvation of anyone that will believe. I am firmly convinced that when we will love others more than ourselves, we will see God move in our churches like never before.

Never Underestimate the Power of Exhortation

A barrage of cards of encouragement arrived in the mailbox everyday, and mail time became the highlight of my day. It seemed that every time that I would begin to get discouraged, just the right card from the right person would brighten my world. The Bible tells us to encourage one another (see Hebrews 10:25), and I was so glad that people from all walks of life, from varying church backgrounds took time to think of me and send an expression of their care and concern for my situation. Many days those cards helped me through a difficult day.

Finances poured in from everywhere meeting all our medical obligations. Family, friends, and churches were determined that my medical expenses would not put Ronda and I in a financial bind. We received several gifts from people that we had never met, but who had heard about what we were going through. Our church, Grace Tabernacle, gave us an offering totaling several thousand dollars to pay for things our insurance would not cover.

Other churches in the area sent us checks to be used for whatever was needed. Graceland Baptist Church, where my friend Steve Marcum pastored, called and offered whatever financial assistance I might need to pay any balance during my hospitalization. The local church community immersed us with a practical outpouring of compassion. Ronda and I were absolutely overwhelmed and relieved knowing we had one less thing on our overloaded minds.

The Tide Begins to Turn

We were given a six-week window until a return trip to the hospital was needed for another CT scan. I was assured by the doctors that by that visit the tests would show that the disease had spread to my liver and lungs, and if I chose to look into the chemotherapy options again, a proposed regiment of drugs would be discussed.

Every day had become precious and I wanted to enjoy it to the fullest. I love to preach and was determined to do so. I arrived home on Tuesday and immediately begin to prepare to preach Wednesday night. I had a large incision in my abdomen and was adjusting to the urostomy bag on my right side so I decided to make an adjustment in my normal preaching attire. I purchased a couple of jogging suits, put on a tee shirt and tennis shoes, tucked my bible under my arm and headed for church determined to preach as long as I had breath and could still sit up and take nourishment. The church purchased a large blue recliner and put it on the platform for me to sit in until it was time to deliver the evening message. This arrangement might not have been very traditional, but it sure worked for me.

During the six-week window, the congregation at Grace Tabernacle met every night to pray for my healing. No matter what kind of day I had experienced, those nightly meetings became a life sustaining experience for me. Nightly, my spirit was inundated with God's concern for me through the people as they prayed for me. Romans 10:17 says, "All faith comes by hearing and hearing by the Word of God." Faith for my healing would arise in me as friends read aloud the promises of God concerning my situation.

As Dickens once wrote, "It was the best of times and the worst of times." Daily I went from the battlefield to the spiritual hospital, from times of struggle to times of refreshing. I discovered, as the Apostle Paul, that power is perfected in weakness and that when we are weak is when we are strong (see 2 Corinthians 12:9,10). Invitations to speak began to pour in from Baptist, Christian, Independent and Assemblies of God churches in the area. To my utmost amazement, I witnessed God's power displayed everywhere I went and operated under the greatest anointing I had ever experienced. I would have a tough day, feeling so badly that it was hard to pray and prepare to minister. And then when I would go to church and open my mouth to speak, a rush of the presence of God flowed that I knew was completely His doing and not my own.

It was such a paradox to me that during the toughest time of my life, God would use me the most. I discovered that the anointing of God is all about Him and His desire to help people and very little about the vessel He is using. We are like a hose from which the Spirit flows. We just need to keep our hose free from any spiritual debris that would hinder the flow of the Holy Spirit.

The Door You Close May Be the Door God Wants You to Walk Through

The six-week window closed faster than I anticipated. I was not looking forward to the CT scan and its revelations, but somehow I found the courage to make the trip to Indianapolis and hand my body over to the doctors to be poked and prodded again. I determined not to let anything get to me. I guarded my emotions to fortify myself against negative doctors' reports because I found that if my emotions got involved, I was ineffective in making a spiritual decision. I wanted to make all decisions based on what I felt the Holy Spirit was saying to me, not on the dictates of my emotions.

Though I was braced for the worst, the CT scan revealed the cancer had not spread to the liver and lungs, and the doctors were encouraged that the disease had not spread as rapidly as they had anticipated. I was none the less assured that it was only a matter of time before the natural progression of the disease would reach those vital organs. The inevitable would not be avoided, only delayed.

While the doctors were discussing what my medical options were, I could not help but to think about the six-week season of prayer that my congregation had engaged in on my behalf. *Was it possible that those nights of intercession had stopped the progression of the disease? Was it within the realm of hope that God was intervening on my behalf and touching me with His life altering power?*

I felt a great sense of relief that things were, at least, not getting worse. A stalemate is better than an advance of the enemy anytime. Dr. Rowland, my urologist, wanted me to meet with Dr. Bruce Roth, an oncologist who specialized in cancer of the urinary tract to consider chemotherapy options. The FDA had approved some drugs to be tested on bladder cancer, and the hospital was going to be a part of a nationwide program to study the effects of these drugs on terminally ill patients or on patients with a prognosis of having less than a year to live.

Chemotherapy, for a multitude of reasons, had very little appeal to me. I had conducted too many funerals of cancer victims that had received little help from the oncologists' valiant efforts to stop the spread of this deadly disease through a regiment of chemotherapy. Most of us have made predetermined decisions about what we would or would not do in the event of contracting a serious illness. Too often those decisions are based on a view from the outside looking in instead of the inside looking out. Though I had said, "Never" to ever consider taking chemotherapy, my circumstances caused my *never attitude* to change.

My biggest concern was what effects the drugs would have on my ability to preach. In viewing my options, I determined that I would rather have six months of quality time able to perform my duties as a pastor than have one year of existence lying around in bed overwhelmed by the effects of the chemotherapy. I did not want to do anything that would steal any quality time from me.

Anyone combating cancer will tell you that making decisions on what kind and how much of any treatment offered is a gut wrenching battle. Your decisions not only affect you, but everyone around you. So many lives, your spouse, children, and friends are drastically altered by whatever decision you make. And until a decision is made, sifting through all the options consumes every waking moment.

After being worn down by the constant encouragement of family and friends for me to meet with Dr. Bruce Roth, I reluctantly agreed to at least hear what he had to offer. By that time in my fight with cancer, I had developed a rather dim view of hospitals and doctors. The prospects of a three-hour drive combined with a lengthy wait in a doctor's office to meet with someone I really did not want to see produced a preacher with a nasty attitude. But the thing that I dreaded the most was hearing, once again, how bad my condition was.

My expectations of hearing a negative report were fulfilled as I listened to one of Dr. Roth's interns go over my medical chart. She explained that the possible chemo regiment would not cure me, but only give me an uncertain possibility of retarding the growth of the tumors. Case studies had shown that 40% of cancer patients taking the regiment of drugs they wanted to give me had some positive response. I was assured that, within the realm of the medical field, that the chemotherapy was my first and last option for treatment. If I decided not to take the drugs, or if I took them and had no response, my life span would be measured in months, not years.

My foul disposition heightened. The visit was everything and more I had imagined it would be, and I was on the verge of leaving when Dr. Roth entered the examination room. With no fanfare, and after a simple introduction, Dr. Roth asked me two questions. One, "Would you like to be able to preach another year? And two, "Would you like to see your son play another year of baseball? Both, he explained, could be possible if I would give chemo a chance.

The regiment Dr. Roth prescribed would have some very serious side effects, but in his medical opinion, the drugs would not interfere with my pastoral duties. Dr. Bruce Roth could sell an ice cube to an Eskimo and his endearing personality and positive attitude caused me to totally change my perspective. There would be no guarantees, but a 40% chance was better than no chance at all.

The drugs that Dr. Roth wanted to give me had been proven effective in treatment of some types of cancer but had never been used in the treatment of bladder cancer. He wanted me to be a part of a study group of 24 patients who would be given a combination of three drugs that would be compared to other patients receiving differing combinations of other recently approved FDA drugs. Resulting responses would be compared, and hopefully, something that would help enhance the length and quality of life of cancer patients would emerge from the studies. I could not help but feel as we were being asked to become guinea pigs in the medical field's quest for new knowledge.

The regiment required patient to receive chemo intravenously in six different five-day hospital stays. I would arrive at the cancer ward on Monday morning, get hooked up, and receive the cancer fighting drugs and other medicines to combat the side effects of the chemo. On Friday evenings after each five-day stay, I would return home to rest and prepare for the next round of chemo 16 days later.

April through July, my life revolved around a 21-day cycle, 5 days in the hospital and 16 days at home. The only positive was that after two sessions, the doctors would be able to determine if the drugs were having any success, and if they were not, the treatment would be stopped. I left Dr. Roth's office with a myriad of things floating through my mind.

Family and friends encouraged me to take the chemo. I despised the thought of giving my body over to the doctors again and putting my hope in their abilities, but the impassioned pleas from those who loved me started to wear on my resistance. Night after night, prayer session after prayer session, I agonized over what decision to make. I wanted the peace of God to be my umpire on this matter (see Col. 3:15), but finding that peace became a lengthy ordeal.

One factor that heavily influenced my decision was a Trinity Broadcasting telecast interviewing several pastors and spiritual leaders who had overcome cancer. As each one shared their ordeals of surgery, chemotherapy and radiation, as well as, the emotional and spiritual battles they had survived, I began to weep as I listened to someone who could relate to the feelings of my infirmities.

As those pastors and spiritual leaders shared their experiences with chemo, each proclaimed that they had continued to minister during treatment. Hope began to well up within me as I saw survivors of the very disease I was battling proclaim victory on the other side of treatment.

After several times of intense prayer, and weighing every factor over and over, I decided to take the chemotherapy. The best case scenario would give me some more quality time, and the worst case scenario would be that I had at least exhausted all my options for a possible medical cure.

Before chemo could begin, the tumors in my bladder would have to be measured so that a standard of the effectiveness of the drugs could be determined. If the tumors diminished in size, the doctors would know the drugs were working. If the tumors did not respond or continued to enlarge, the treatments would be determined to be ineffective and stopped. A cystoscope performed three days before my first scheduled chemo session revealed three golf ball-sized tumors in my bladder. The tumors were measured and photographed and those pictures became the *markers* that would determine the effectiveness of the chemotherapy. My journey into the unknown of chemotherapy was just beginning.

CHAPTER 3

Confronting My Situation

Even though it is inevitable that we all are one day going to die, having a time frame placed on that inevitable event brings a stark realism that instantly sobers you. The realism I faced that cold February afternoon sitting alone in my office was unless something supernatural happened to me, I was going to die. As is the case with so many decisions in life when the going gets tough and it looks like it is all over, we must decide what course of action we are going to take. Will we give into the voices of despondency that scream in our head and the video effects that our eyes see, or will we rise to fight the good fight of faith? (see 1 Tim. 5:12)

With simply willful determination and no emotions, I decided that I was going to fight the good fight of faith to my final breath. Either God was going to help me, or I was going to die, but either way, whatever time I had left was not going to be lived feeling sorry for myself and under the control of discouragement and fear. I needed a battle plan to refer to on a daily basis to keep focused on the truth and the reality of the God I serve.

Almost daily, either by personal visit, mail or telephone, I received videotapes and articles about alternative cancer treatment or pamphlets about diets that fight cancer cells. As this stuff piled up on my desk in front of me, the thought occurred, *It would take me a year to go through all this stuff, and I only have six months to live. I am not going to spend the bulk of my remaining time wading through this pile hoping that there is a cure hidden somewhere in all of this.*

The Bible presents Jesus in many different reflections of the Godhead. He is the exact representation of God according to Hebrews 1:3. If you want to know what God is like, simply look to the Jesus in the Gospels. Jesus is the exact representation of the Father. As I looked at all the envelopes, brochures, books, and tapes laying on my desk, I wondered if there was anyone who could really relate to what I was going through. I did not need theory or experimentation. I needed reality, someone who had gone through what I was currently battling and had survived. Jesus is touched with the feeling of our infirmities (Hebrews 4:15), and on that day, not only did I need a savior that was touched with the feelings of my infirmities, but also I needed encouragement from someone that had fought cancer and won.

As I began to sort through the pile of information on my desk, I came across *Healed of Cancer,* a little book by Dodie Osteen. As I picked the book from the pile on my desk, a flicker of hope, something I desperately needed, ignited in my spirit. I sat down on my couch and began to read this fascinating story of her initial diagnosis, ensuing battle, and ultimate victory over liver cancer. The thing that most impressed me was the battle plan she devised containing scriptures and attitudes of the heart that she reviewed daily to keep her faith strong in God's ultimate victory.

Please understand what I am about to say because I believe it is true. Unless you have gone through something, though you may have knowledge concerning it, you have little to say to someone who is going through something you have never experienced. I was constantly bombarded by well meaning people telling me what they thought I should do. Reality for all of us is that we really do not know what we will do in any given situation until we are there. I found myself, during my battle with cancer, doing things that I had once proclaimed that I would never do.

This is one reason that Jesus had to come to earth as a human being (see John 1:14). He had to be touched with the feelings of our infirmities if He was to be able to fulfill His present day office as intercessor (see Hebrews 7:25). Because He has gone before us in all the realities of life's experiences, He can come to the aid of those who are struggling. I found myself gravitating to people who had already battled cancer and alienated from all the theories of those who did not have firsthand experience with what I was going through.

I placed my trashcan beside my desk and with one swoop eliminated the pile of material on my desk. I retrieved those materials born from real experiences and placed them next to my bible. I needed a battle plan and it was going to have to come from the Word of God interspersed with the real experiences of those that had faced cancer and survived.

I sat down at my word processor that February afternoon and the following thoughts, attitudes, and scriptures became my daily battle plan that sustained me. The battle plan was birthed from the word of God, my own failures to that point in battling cancer, and the testimonies and successes of others that had overcome cancer. The plan included the followed:

Remain positive. Negativity will destroy you.

During my nine-day stay in the hospital, the only news we heard was bad news. I had gone into surgery to have my cancerous bladder replaced with a neo-bladder, but came out of surgery with a urostomy pouch. Because of grossly positive lymph node involvement surrounding my bladder, a prognosis that the disease had most likely invaded my liver and lungs gave a life expectancy of two months to a year. Believe me, it takes some real creative thinking to find anything positive in that prognosis.

When we arrived home, we began to receive phone calls and visits from family and friends who wanted to know the seriousness of my condition. Day after day, our conversations were consumed with relating the negative prognosis we were given. Phone call after phone call, visit after visit focused on the negative. A depression set in like I had never experienced.

Every night, I would wake up around 3 a.m. with the same dream. Pallbearers, representing both sides of my family and close friends, carried me down the aisle of the church. I was overwhelmed by the idea that I was going to die. One evening during that time, Ronda came running down the stairs to the couch where I was sleeping and threw herself on me and began to weep uncontrollably with the thought of my impending death.

I made a determination that night that Ronda and I were going to get out of the realm of the negative and get into the realm of the positive. We both determined that we were not going to give any expression to negativism. We realized that positive confession was not going to make the cancer go away, but positive confession was going to help our attitudes tremendously.

The Bible tells us we are not to be conformed to this world, shaped by outward circumstances and influences, but to be transformed by the renewing of our mind (see Romans 12:2). I understood the principle that the Holy Spirit speaks to our renewed born-again spirit, not our unregenerate head. I desperately needed head by-pass surgery. I needed to quit listening to my head and to start listening to what the Spirit of God was telling me.

Ronda and I determined from that day forth, we were going to respond positively to everyone that asked about my condition. We were not going to lie but to respond in such a manner that kept us focused on what we believed God was going to do and not what the doctors said was inevitable.

We could not believe what a change speaking positively made. I found that speaking to myself more and listening to my head less brought hope and life. I could not sit around all day and dwell on negative things and not expect it to drain all the life out of me. To stay positive, you must devise a plan and determine to carry it out.

Let the peace of God be your greatest source of guidance.

In a struggle with cancer, there will be many important decisions to be made. Advice to battle cancer came from all sources and every conceivable avenue. Some close friends told me that seeking any more medical treatment would show a lack of faith and would cause me to lose my connection to God's healing power. Others told me to seek every available medical treatment whether FDA approved or not. Friends who had read articles on diets encouraged me to change my eating habits. Relatives who cared deeply for me told me of experimental treatments available in Mexico and Europe. I was flooded with information and at a total loss as what to do.

Many times in life we cannot see the forest for the trees, especially when our vision is completely blocked by the large oak that is so large it encompasses all we can see. We do not know what to do, but God does. The scripture in James 1:5 proclaims, "If any man lacks wisdom, let him ask God who gives freely." It was my experience that I did not know what to do or what avenue to take until the exact moment the decision had to be made. I learned to live on a daily basis, asking God's guidance for that day's decision, and not to concern myself about future events. I took to heart the admonition of the scripture that tells me to take no thought about tomorrow because each day has enough trouble of its own (Matthew 6:34).

In the struggle with cancer, I discovered that you must do whatever you feel peace in your heart to do. There will be voices screaming everywhere, and the one that screams the loudest might not be the right one. I found that following only those things that were birthed of peace produced life.

Never sit around and feel sorry for yourself.

Pity never wins. Over the years as I have pastored people, I have counseled many who have struggled with depression and discouragement. Some I have been able to help, and others I could not reach. I knew that one of the major battles I was going to face was the strong desire to give into depression and discouragement. Why do I have to go through this? I have faithfully served God in ministry for nearly 20 years and this is my reward? These questions dogged me constantly.

Over the years I had observed that those who give into depression usually begin my regressing or pulling away from others. They like to stay home, pull the blinds, and invite into their living room all the little devils that have been harassing them. If you invite the devil in for a pity party, he will bring all the bells and whistles. The devil always brings old home movies highlighting the times you have felt rejected and unloved by people and God.

The commercials in the home movies stress how dire your situation is, and how there is no hope, and that you might as well give up. An afternoon pity party in the company of devils usually entails a double or triple feature. Every negative thought is played over and over, each time allowing the scenario to get worse and worse. The end result is that pity and sorrow become your constant companions. You lose all your strength and energy as the weight of your circumstances, defined by demonic forces, crushes you with waves of despair and despondency. Your isolation separates you from anything encouraging or godly. Pity has become your master.

I came to the conclusion that the answer was not in my head. There is nothing rational about cancer. I began to force myself out of the house and among people. I knew I could either feel badly lying around the house, or I could feel badly mingling with church friends and family. My countenance began to change by my being around people and hearing positive comments. I understood the seriousness of time alone for prayer and meditation, but I stopped sitting around the house thinking about my condition. I jumped into the flow of life and found the battle with self-pity one that I could overcome.

Don't allow your imagination to run wild.

The Bible tells us that we live in the flesh, but we do not war according to the flesh (2 Corinthians 10:3-5). The weapons of our warfare are divinely powerful for the destruction of fortresses. These strongholds are vain imaginations, foolish speculations, and every lofty thing that exalts itself against the true knowledge of God. We must remember that all communication with the Lord comes from the Spirit of God that reveals things to our spirits.

The Holy Spirit will illuminate to us what the Spirit of God is saying. Our head plays no role in this communication. Our spirits will feed our head one dose of reality at a time. But transformation comes to any person as their mind is renewed as the Spirit feeds it the truth of God. I had to learn to take negative thoughts captive and cast them down.

After casting down the negative thoughts, I had to speak to my mind the truth about my condition, speaking to myself more and listening to myself less. One thing that I found that helped greatly was finding a quiet place to talk out loud to myself. I had to speak to myself louder than my mind was talking to me. Some of the best sermons I have ever preached were to myself as I cast down vain imaginations and foolish speculations and replaced them with the all-powerful Word of God.

Do not focus all your attention and energies on yourself.

It is our natural tendency when fighting a giant like cancer to focus all our attention and energies on ourselves. However, when we get our mind exclusively on ourselves, and our needs, we begin to weaken. There are all kinds of natural laws that govern the universe. The law of gravity tells us that what goes up must come down. All of us have discovered that no two pieces of matter can occupy the same place at the same time. We all have experienced a knock or two on our heads that has made that law a painful reality.

Spiritual laws are no different than natural laws. There are God-given principles that govern life in the spirit realm. One of those laws is the law of sowing and reaping. Luke, the apostle tells us that if we give, it will be given back to us in such a good measure that we will not be able to contain it (see Luke 6:38).

One of the biggest mistakes I made early on in my illness was that I focused too much attention on my own need and too little on the needs of those around me. Desperately, desiring for the strangle hold of depression to be broken, I asked the Lord why I could not shake its powerful grip. Like so many times during my ordeal, the Holy Spirit illuminated my mind to see that I was not giving anything out. If nothing is being planted, there can never be any harvest.

With this revelation, I decided to throw myself into ministry with both barrels blazing. Our church services were not going to revolve around my sickness, but the needs of the congregation were going to take precedence over mine. I determined to focus my attention on others that were hurting and give what I could to them. I found that as I prayed and ministered to others, I felt dramatically different about my own circumstances. As I gave ministry to others, the Holy Spirit ministered peace and encouragement to me in a far greater fashion than I had experienced by focusing my attention upon myself. I found that if you give out of your need, God causes good things to come your way.

You cannot lie around sick.

You must do everything possible to stay active and productive. You must not give into the sickness. Believe me, I know this sounds harsh, but this truth is forged in the fires of adversity. In 1996, I had two major surgeries, six separate five-day chemotherapy treatments, and spent fifty days in the hospital. Much of what I faced was dealing with thoughts telling me to just give in, to lie down, and to take it easy.

I made a mental commitment to be up and around as much as possible. I learned how to pace myself because the chemo took a terrible toll on my physical strength. I would work at the office until my strength was gone. Afternoon naps became a necessity.

My chemotherapy was on a 21-day cycle, arriving at the hospital early Monday morning, getting hooked up to an IV and taking the drugs until Friday afternoon. I would be allowed to go home for 16 days while my body recovered and then start the cycle all over again.

It always amazed me that the day I felt the worst was also the day I had the most to do. Sunday was a tough day. Most Sundays during the chemo treatments, I found myself nauseous and physically weak. Every round of chemo left me a little weaker and with less resilience to bounce back. During the first four rounds of treatment, I never missed a service. I would sit in the blue recliner near the platform to conserve my strength for preaching and ministry to the church.

It was the Sunday morning after my 5th round of chemo that I hit a wall. When Ronda called for me to get up, I told her that I just could not make it. I was too sick. I felt that surely everyone would understand that I, of all people, deserved to lie around and take it easy. As I snuggled under the covers, the Holy Spirit quietly spoke these words to my heart, "So this is where you draw the line." "This is how sick you have to be to lie down and quit?" "If this is where you draw the line, the devil will keep you at this place and render you ineffective." As this sobering piece of revelation hit me, I jumped out of bed and headed for the shower. I had come too far to lie down and quit.

Too many people facing adversity lie down and quit way too early in the fracas. If you tell the devil where the line is, he will manipulate circumstances to keep you there at that point of pain or discomfort or mental anguish. You must determine that as long as you have physical strength, you must stay productive. This attitude of the heart is more for your benefit than for the benefit for others.

Stay mentally strong by renewing your mind on a daily basis.

Allow your spirit to renew your mind on a daily basis. There is something about the 24-hour cycle of life that many of us have never fully comprehended. If we understand that we cannot live on yesterday's food or water, why do we think we can live on yesterday's spiritual revelations?

If I did not renew my mind daily by feeding on the Word of God and His promises, discouragement and depression would begin to creep out of the shadows to engulf me in darkness. Your mind will begin to waver and you will be prone to believe the negative. But if you keep your spirit strong, it will speak to your head spiritual realities and bring it back to the realm of faith. You must keep your spirit strong or your head will waver. James 1:8 warns us about the danger of being double minded. The Word of God must become the source of your strength. You must read, meditate, and confess the realities of God's word on a daily basis.

In spite of what your eyes see, your ears hear, and your thoughts proclaim, you must have absolute faith that the Word of God cannot lie. The writer of Hebrews 10:23 cautions us, "...to hold fast the confession of our faith without wavering, for He who promised is faithful." Your grip on God is your faith. His grip on you is His grace. As you meditate on His word, your grip on God will increase. You must hear the right things even if you have to read the Word out loud so you can hear yourself proclaim words of faith inspired by the Holy Spirit.

State your case before God.

One thing every born-again believer must fully realize is that he has access to the throne room of God (see Hebrews 10:19-20). We have access because God personally made himself responsible for our sinful condition in Adam. He made Jesus, who knew no sin, become sin on our behalf so that we might be able to attain right standing with God. We serve a savior who is touched with the feelings of our infirmities and invites us to the throne room to find mercy in our time of need. Through the death, burial, and resurrection of Jesus, all the barriers to God have been removed, and we have been granted entrance presenting ourselves to God, holy, blameless, and beyond reproach, wondrously transformed by our faith in his promise.

Isaiah 43:25-26 encourages us to state our case before God. I must admit when I came across this powerful concept, I found it hard to grasp how a human being could actually relate to God in such a powerful way. As I was praying one afternoon, the story of Moses contending with God concerning the Hebrews and Abraham contending with God over the cities of Sodom and Gomorrah flashed through my mind. I did not need to guide Israel or intercede over the fate of thousands in those cities, but I reasoned, if these men contended with God, so could I.

During my daily prayer times, I began to state my case before God. I would cry out to the Lord that 17 years earlier He had led me to pioneer an Assembly of God church in an area that had been devoid of anything that hinted of Pentecostalism. For 17 years I had proclaimed Him as a healer of sick bodies. I had conducted healing crusades in the church and had seen many miracles. I would contend with the Lord and ask him how my death would glorify His name and in the area where I pastored? I asked him what would it look like if I, the pastor of the local Pentecostal church who proclaimed God as healer, died little by little in front of the entire community?

The prospect of physically deteriorating in full view of our small closed community was a scenario that I told God I did not want that to happen. As I would pray, I would ask God to allow me to live and not die. I asked that He would reveal to all that observed my condition that God was indeed a healer.

I would tell the Lord that my son, sixteen at the time, needed me. My wife and daughter needed me. I was too young to die. There was too much stuff for me to do here. I told the Lord that I completely understood that Heaven was a wonderful place, but it was my desire to further His kingdom here on earth. I would promise the Lord that if he would heal me, I would continue to preach the Gospel and minister to broken people through the power of His name.

I truly established in my heart the scriptural admonition that whatever things you desire, believe you shall receive them and they shall be yours (see John 14:13-14). I wanted to live for the glory of God, to remain with my family, and to continue to preach the Gospel. I wanted to choose life and not death and reveal to all that were watching my condition that the God I served was indeed a mighty God. I cannot describe to any person the closeness I developed with the Lord as I prayed. It was like for the first time, I was aware of the close knit relationship a man could have with God. I felt as if for the first time in my life, my will became intertwined with His.

Examine your heart regularly and keep it pure with God and others.

You cannot deal with the *Why me?* question 24 hours a day. The *Why me?* question is simply answered by understanding man's condition in Adam after the fall, or the introduction of sin. Adam's sin affected every realm of nature and humanity. Sickness is part of the package we all inherited through our ancestor, Adam.

Jesus, in addressing man's condition in Adam came to earth and exhibited total dominion over sickness and disease. Sickness is a result of the fall of man and Jesus was God's response to man's fall. He came as a savior to save us from the consequences of sin (see I John 3:8). There is healing in Jesus' name.

I found it very easy to fall into guilt and condemnation over my condition. I constantly asked the questions, "Am I in some kind of sin that brought sickness to me?" "Have I failed God in some areas of my life and this is the punishment for it?" "Is God trying to get my attention about something?" I felt that if I could answer the *Why me* question, everything else would fall into place.

The devil's main weapon against us is accusation. The devil is described as the accuser of the brethren before God day and night (see Revelation 12:10). Our access to God comes through the avenue of the righteousness Jesus purchased for us. It does not come through obedience to the law.

If you are born-again, you are as righteous as you will ever get. You have right standing with God through your faith that Jesus' death, burial, and resurrection satisfied all the legal demands of a holy God. You have a legal right to stand before God, not through the means of your own goodness, but fully confident that Jesus reconciled you back to the Father through his fleshly body to present you holy and blameless and beyond reproach.

I came to the spiritual reality that the devil wanted to separate me from the Father through accusation. The devil wanted me to be offended with God because I was sick and it was taking so long to get well. I had thought, *What kind of God would allow this to happen? I didn't deserve this.* Without being fully aware of it, my relationship with God was slowly being poisoned and tainted because of listening to the accusations of the devil.

If there is one person in your life you want a good relationship with it is God. You cannot get offended with the source of your help. Subtly, the devil was trying to separate me from the One who holds the power of life and death.

Physical problems affect every area of our lives. No matter how close you try to walk with God, sickness makes it difficult to focus on spiritual realities. We soon become moved only by how we feel. It is easy for attitudes to go south and faith and hope to dissipate. My going before the Father and allowing the Holy Spirit to examine my heart to see if there was any wicked way in me, allowed His blood to cleanse me from all defilement.

Your hope is in God and those you love. You must keep those relationships open, clean and pure because everything you need for life is found there. You cannot allow how you feel physically to contaminate the pipeline from which life sustaining sustenance flows.

Even when the physical illness begins to wear on you with the overwhelming temptation to give in to it, you will find God is always faithful. I wavered at times almost to the point of giving up, but God would arrange someone or some thought to bring me back to the place of faith. There will be times when we waver in our minds, but our spirits must stay full of faith for our healing.

CHAPTER 4

Daily Living According to Scripture

The Word of God must become your life as you battle cancer. The answers you so desperately need, the encouragement to cope, and the strength to overcome are found in God's word. 1 Corinthians 2:10-16 tells us we have the mind of Christ.

Too often, too many among us believe that the answer for everything is found within the realm of rationality. Nothing about disease can be figured out in the head. You can fix a flat tire, or bake a cake using the carnal mind, but if you need something miraculous, such as healing, the answers are spiritual ones. These answers can only come to your spirit as it is in communion with the Spirit of God.

We must allow scripture to determine who we are. All faith comes by hearing and hearing by the word of God (see Romans 10:17). Faith is your connection to God and the more the Word of God becomes alive in you, the more your faith will grow. The Word became my life.

I came to the awareness that Jesus was wounded for my transgressions, bruised for my iniquities, the chastening for my well being had fallen on Him and by His stripes I am healed (see Isaiah 53:5). God is no respecter of persons. If Jesus is the same today, yesterday and forever then that same Jesus that healed disease on the shores of Galilee could heal me today (see Hebrews 13:8).

The Word of God has to dwell in you and you must speak to yourself constantly concerning the truth as recorded in the scriptures. You must stand on the truth that you have bold access to God through the blood of Jesus and must go to the throne room of God and confidently state your case before the Father.

Many evenings in the sanctuary of the church, I would enter into His presence and state my case and contend with God about my condition. "I do not want to die but live and proclaim the glory of the Lord!" I would cry. "My wife, family, and church need me."

The Lord is good and a very present help in times of trouble. As I meditated on the Word, I became aware that the same Spirit that raised Jesus from the dead was working in me and giving life to my mortal body (see Romans 8:11). It began to burn in my spirit that when I prayed whatever things I asked for I would receive if I prayed in faith. I developed a rock solid confidence in the integrity of the Word of God. I had to learn to not throw away my confidence, but to continue to believe, so my faith would open to me all the things God had purchased for me in Christ.

It is imperative that you get control of your thinking. You must take every thought captive to the obedience of Christ. Negative thinking is detrimental to developing faith. You must force yourself to think on the truth of God, not in doctor's reports. As Joshua asked the Hebrews, "Whose report will you believe?" I too had to choose to believe the report of the Word of God and not doctors.

Pride has no place in a battle with cancer. I knew that there would be times when others would have to carry me. On a regular basis, the leadership of the church prayed for me. I stood on the promise of the Word of God that the effectual, fervent prayers of righteous men would play a part in the healing process (see James 5:16). Everywhere I went I opened myself to righteous people of God who wanted to lay hands on me and pray for my recovery.

Daily I had to check the condition of my heart. It is so easy to allow discouragement and wrong attitudes to creep in. I asked the Lord to examine the condition of my heart and deal with anything that would defile and keep His life-giving spirit from flowing through me. I found that the negativity that was always lurking in the background was forced to stay there as I asked the Lord to allow the words of my mouth and the meditations of my heart to be acceptable in His sight.

Our lives are truly hidden with God in Christ. Nothing would calm the raging storm within like the nightly sessions that I had with the Lord in the sanctuary of the church. It was there that I presented myself to God and asked for His Spirit to cleanse my entire body, soul, and spirit.

During every preceding 24 hours anxiety, doubt, fear, and worry, began to try to assert dominance over me. Nightly these attitudes had to be confronted and taken care of according to the Word of God. Demonic spirits that had been competing for my attention all day had to be driven away as I proclaimed my intentions and stated my case before God. As I would leave the church each evening, I would feel cleansed, much like a physical shower refreshes the body, but fully aware that I would have to repeat this process again the following evening. The following scriptures I reviewed on a daily basis:

Psalms 103:1-3 Bless (affectionately, gratefully praise) the Lord, O my soul; and all that is (deepest) within me, bless his holy name! Bless (affectionately, gratefully praise) the Lord, O my soul; and forget not (one of) all his benefits. Who forgives all (every one of) your iniquities, Who heals all (each one) your diseases.

Isaiah 53:5 But he was wounded for our transgressions, He was bruised for our guilt and iniquities; the chastisement (needful to obtain) peace and well being for us was upon Him and with the stripes (that wounded) Him we are healed and made whole.

Isaiah 43:25-26 I, even I am he who blots out and cancels your transgressions, for my own sake, and I will not remember your sins. Put me in remembrance (remind me of your merits); let us plead and argue together. Set forth your case, that you may be justified.

Matthew 4:23 and healing every disease and every weakness and infirmity among the people. And He went about all Galilee, teaching in their synagogues and preaching the good news (Gospel) of the kingdom

Mark 10:51-52 And Jesus said to him, what do you want me to do for you? And the blind man said to him, Master, let me receive my sight. And Jesus said to him, go your way; your faith has healed you. And at once he received his sight and accompanied Jesus on the road.

James 5:13-14 Is anyone among you sick? He should call in the church elders (the spiritual guides). And they should pray over him, anointing him with oil in the Lord's name. And the prayer (that is) of faith will save him who is sick, and the Lord will restore him; and if he has committed sins, he will be forgiven.

Psalms 118:17 *I shall not die but live, and shall declare the works and recount the illustrious acts of God.*

Luke 6:38 *Give and (gifts) will be given to you; good measure, pressed down, shaken together, and running over, will they pour into (the pouch formed by) the bosom (of your robe and used as a bag). For with the measure you deal out (with the measure you use when you confer benefits on others), it will be measured back to you.*

Colossians 3:16 *Let the word (spoken by) Christ (the messiah) have its home (in your hearts and minds) and dwell in you in (all its) richness; as you teach and admonish and train one another in all insight and intelligence and wisdom (in spiritual things, and as you sing) psalms and hymns and spiritual songs, making melody to God with (His) grace in your hearts.*

Nahum 1:7 *The Lord is good, a strength and stronghold in the day of trouble; He knows (recognizes, has knowledge of and understands) those who take refuge and trust in Him.*

Joshua 21:45 *There failed no part of any good thing which the Lord had promised to the house of Israel; all came to pass.*

Romans 8:11 *And if the Spirit of Him who raised up Jesus form the dead dwells in you (then) He who raised up Christ Jesus from the dead will also restore to life your mortal (short-lived, perishable) bodies through His Spirit Who dwells in you.*

2 Corinthians 1:20 *For as many as are the promises of God; they all find their Yes (answer) in Him (Christ). For this reason we also utter the Amen (so be it) to God through Him (in His person and by His agency) to the glory of God.*

Matthew 8:2-3 *And behold, a leper came up to Him and prostrating himself, worshiped Him saying, Lord, if you are willing, You are able to cleanse me by curing me. And He reached out His hand and touched him, saying, I am willing; be cleansed by being cured. And instantly his leprosy was cured and cleansed.*

Hebrews 11:6 *But without faith, it is impossible to please and be satisfactory to Him. For whoever would come near to God must (necessarily) believe that God exists and that He is a rewarder of those who earnestly and diligently seek Him (out).*

Psalms 107:20 *He sends forth His Word and heals them and rescues them from the pit and destruction.*

Mark 11:22-24 *And Jesus, replying, said to them, have faith in God (constantly). Truly, I tell you, whoever says to this mountain. Be lifted up and thrown into the sea and does not doubt at all in his heart but believes that what he says will take place. It will be done for him. For this reason I am telling you, whatever you ask for in prayer, believe (trust and be confident) that it is granted to you and you will (get it).*

Mark 16:17-18 *And these attesting signs will accompany those who believe; in My name they shall drive out demons; they will speak in new languages; they will pick up serpents; and (even) if they drink anything deadly, it will not hurt them; they will lay their hands on the sick, and they will get well.*

Hebrews 10-23 *So let us seize and hold fast and retain without wavering the hope we cherish and confess and our acknowledgement of it, for He Who promised is reliable (sure) and faithful to His word.*

Hebrews 10:35 *Do not, therefore, fling away your fearless confidence, for it carries a great and glorious compensation of reward.*

I John 5:14 *And this is the confidence (the assurance, the privilege of boldness) which we have in Him; (we are sure) that if we ask anything (make any request) according to His will (in agreement with His own plan), He listens and hears us.*

2 Timothy 1:7 *For God did not give us a spirit of timidity (of cowardice, of craven and cringing and fawning fear), but (He has given us a spirit) of power and of love and of calm and well balanced mind and discipline and self-control.*

2 Corinthians 10:3-6 *For though we walk (live) in the flesh, we are not carrying on our warfare according to the flesh and using mere human weapons. For the weapons of our warfare are not physical (weapons of flesh and blood), but they are mighty before God for the overthrow and destruction of strongholds, (In as much as) we refute arguments and theories and reasonings and every proud and lofty thing that sets itself up against the (true) knowledge of God; and we lead every thought and purpose away captive into the obedience of Christ (the Messiah, the Anointed One).*

Romans 21:1-2 *I appeal to you therefore, brethren and beg of you in view of (all) the mercies of God, to make a decisive dedication of your bodies (presenting all your members and faculties) as a living sacrifice, holy (devoted, concentrated) and well pleasing to God, which is your reasonable (rational, intelligent) service and spiritual worship. Do not be conformed (fashioned after and adapted to its external, superficial customs), to this world (this age), but be transformed (changed) by the (entire) renewal of your mind (by its ideals and its new attitude) so that you may prove (for yourselves) what is the good and acceptable and perfect will of God, even the thing which is good and acceptable and perfect (in His sight for you).*

Jude 1:20 *But you, beloved, build yourselves up (founded) on your most holy faith (make progress, rise like an edifice higher and higher) praying in the Holy Spirit.*

Proverbs 4:23 *Keep and guard your heart with all vigilance and above all that you guard. For out of it flow springs of life.*

Psalms 139:23-24 *Search me (thoroughly), O God, and know my heart! Try me and know my thoughts. And see if there is any wicked or hurtful way in me, and lead me in the way everlasting.*

Jeremiah 17:9-10 *The heart is deceitful above all things, and it is exceedingly perverse and corrupt and severely, mortally sick! Who can know it (perceive, understand, be acquainted with his own heart and mind)? I the Lord search the mind, even to give to every man according to his ways, according to the fruit of his doings.*

Psalms 19:14 *Let the words of my mouth and the meditation of my heart be acceptable in your sight, O Lord, my (firm impenetrable) Rock and my Redeemer.*

CHAPTER 5

Controlling Your Mind

Every day in the United States people are told by doctors that they have a terminal disease. When I heard the word "terminal" from my doctor, I felt a great cloud of darkness attempt to envelop me. But darkness can only encroach where there is no light. Darkness is the absence of light. Satan, before he can gain control of any area of our lives, must first remove the glorious light of Jesus Christ from surrounding us.

Sickness in the body has a profound effect on a person's spirit. Since the body has been designed by God to express what is in the spirit of man, a sick body, already at odds with the spirit because of the sin of Adam, wants to revolt against any prompting of the spirit and focus all attention on its weakness. The flesh wants every thought to be on its treatment and care. The mind wants to go along with the body because of it's carnal nature, and the two team up to overcome the influence of the spirit. Darkness begins to set in because in the carnal mind or the physical man there are no answers.

It is necessary that a person understand that the enemy wants to control your thinking and consume you with great darkness and shut out all light that the Holy Spirit wants to shine on your condition. Beware of the following tactics of the enemy.

The enemy always wants you to *REGRESS*, go back or change, your spiritual pattern of pressing into God. He wants you to give up by painting a bleak picture in your mind. If you are going to succeed, the first thing that you must resolve in your mind is that you cannot allow thinking that tells you to go back or regress to a previous level of spirituality.

When you are battling sickness, there is sometimes an overwhelming temptation to sit around and regress into a pattern of thinking that tells you not to push yourself. I found that one of the keys to overcoming negative thinking patterns was to push myself to do things that my mind was telling me was too difficult for me to accomplish. When I was taking chemotherapy, I discovered that I could lie on the couch and feel badly, or I could be up doing something constructive and feel badly.

Pushing myself daily to do something constructive, got me out of the environment of my own problems and into the realm of the promise of Luke 6:38 that assures us that if we will give, God will give unto us. I found that by giving to others God returned more to me than I could ever give.

Hebrews 11:1 tells us that faith is the substance of the things hoped for and the evidence of the things that we cannot see. Faith brings to us the reality of what we hope for. Hope is future and faith is now. We must constantly have things that we hope for like overcoming physical infirmity, or faith has no object to produce.

Satan wants us to regress from hope and retreat into the hole of human reasoning.

Several times, during visits to the doctors that were treating me, the topic of medication for depression came up. It seemed that the doctors were worried about my mental well being and wanted to help me by prescribing drugs that would ease the mental load I was carrying. I had no desire to retreat or regress into some drug-induced utopia that would numb my abilities to deal with my situation from a spiritual perspective. I felt it imperative to press into God farther than I had ever been instead of regressing into false hope that the drugs would offer.

If you are going to be a person that is pleasing to God, you must diligently and earnestly seek Him. It is pleasing to God when we have problems to diligently seek Him instead of retreating into some drug-induced state rendering us unable to feel anything emotionally or physically. Please keep in mind that I am referring to drugs for depression, not medicines that heal or drugs that alleviate physically suffering. Too many people, when they are battling sickness retreat into the comfort that drugs offer and lose their ability to hear what the Holy Spirit is trying speak to them. You cannot regress, but you must press into God with all your heart.

If you think about regressing or going back, the enemy will present you with all kinds of opportunities to go back. You must constantly do things, dwell on things, and think on things that will cause hope to spring up within you.

Heaven is filled with overcomers. You must not allow sickness to overcome your spirit. The physical cannot overcome the spiritual. You must never lose sight that you are a spirit that has a connection with this earth, your body. Never allow yourself to get to a place where you are more sensitive to the demands of the body than the demands of the spirit.

Psalm 23 tells me that God will prepare a table before me in the presence of my enemies. In your battle with sickness, God has a table that He will prepare for you that is loaded with everything that you need. It may not necessarily have what you want, but it will always have what you need. Your sustenance from God is always ahead, never behind. I found that even in my darkest time, God would give me everything I needed if I would just go to the table He set before me and eat freely. If I would push aside the plate of self-pity and discouragement that I wanted to indulge in and consume His word of encouragement, I would be filled with the life that only His spirit could provide.

Never consume so much of the things of this present world that you lose you appetite for things of God. During times of sickness, avoid the temptation to look to the world and entertain and amuse yourself with its distractions. Those distractions might fill you up for a period of time, but they have no sustenance to them. They cannot sustain you. They will bring you nothing that will empower you to overcome. Only from the table of the Lord, the one He has prepared for you when all hell is raging against you, will you find food that is divinely empowered to enable you to overcome.

Never sit around and think about giving up, no matter how terrible the reports or how badly you feel. Constantly think on the things that will build faith and never lose the hope that you have within you.

The next phase of attack from Satan is *SUPPRESSION*. Inside every believer is the same spirit that raised Christ from the dead. It is God's design to give life to our mortal bodies. We also have the mind of Christ. Every believer has the potential to hear from God and have His life altering power flow through our mortal beings. The enemy knows this and wants to suppress its flow.

If you open up your mind to the lies of the devil, a demonic bulldozer is released to begin to shove you in the direction that your thinking is going. If you are thinking about giving up, satan comes in for the kill.

Coyote hunters have used a tactic for hunting that has proven quite effective. Since the coyote's habitat is so stretched out over uninhabited areas, the hunter must do something to draw the coyote to him. Wily hunters use a recording of a wounded rabbit to entice the coyote to their trap. When the coyote hears the wounded rabbit's cry, he senses an easy dinner is somewhere close and he comes in for the kill. It is the cry of the wounded rabbit that attracts the coyote.

Spiritually, I believe something very similar happens in the realm of the spirit. If you sit around and whine about your condition, if you let everyone know how terrible it is and constantly complain, you are sending out signals that you are wounded and hurt and in dire straits. I believe that there is nothing that attracts evil spirits like a person sending out in the spirit realm that he is wounded and in despair. It is then that the enemy reads your distress signals and comes in for the kill. Never allow the enemy to suppress the power of the Spirit of God that lives within you.

"He who dwells in the secret place of the most high shall abide under the shadow of the Almighty," the psalmist declares. There is a place of safety under the shadow of God. As long as we are there, we are safe. Never allow the enemy to entice you to come out from under that covering. If you come out, you are fair game. No matter what you see with your natural senses, never come out from under the covering of God.

To *SUPPRESS* means to take or put down by force. It also means to check or stop a natural flow. Suppressants are designed to stop something such as appetite, a cough, or pain. The enemy wants to stop or put a check on the natural flow. He will go after your desire to pray, worship, and read the word. If you open up your mind to the possibility of giving up or into sickness, suppression of the spiritual flow of God to combat the negative mental process will stop the life-giving power to sustain you in the battle. Your strength will leave and you will face your greatest enemy, not in the power of the Spirit, but in the power of your own strength. You are no match with your limited power for the onslaught that you will encounter.

It is here that the devil might begin to harass you about your commitment to God and tell you that you have served God in vain. Thoughts may invade your thinking that question why sickness is happening to someone who has tried to serve God faithfully and lived as well as they knew how. As the old proverb tells us, "We cannot keep the birds from circling overhead, but we can keep them from building a nest in our hair," so we must never allow that kind of thinking to take root in our life. We must take a firm stand and never be moved from our position of faith in the integrity of God.

Suppressants are designed to stop or control something. They have no power to cure the condition. If you have a cough and go to the drug store and buy cough syrup, you are purchasing something that will keep you from coughing, not cure your cough.

One of the main reasons that I chose not to take medication for depression is because the medication acts only as a suppressant. The medication would only suppresses the symptoms of the depression not cure them. If you have fear, anxiety, or worry during a bout with sickness, would it not be much better to feast on the Word of God that will cure the symptoms than to take a pill that would only suppress them?

Drugs are one of the major avenues that can open a person for demonic influence. Drugs overwhelm the physical and mental aspects of your personality and keep them from expressing whatever is controlling you. If you are full of fear and anxiety about your condition, the doctor can prescribe a drug that will render you body incapable of expressing the symptom. All the medication is doing is suppressing the problem, not curing it. Nothing has changed but the fact that the drug is more powerful than whatever symptoms are bothering you.

Medication for depression when you are battling physical infirmities can render you ineffective to wage a spiritual war against the problem. It has the potential to affect your ability to pray, hear from God, and most of all, snuff out your drive to push yourself into the realm of the spirit. You have a problem but taking something to suppress it will never get you out of the problem. Anti-depressants will simply allow the problems to remain without the ability to manifest themselves.

If you are battling depression, there is a reason, but problems need to be revealed for what they are in our lives. I hated what depression was doing to me to the degree that I was willing to do whatever was necessary to overcome it. For me, evening sessions of prayer in the sanctuary of the church was the only way I could keep my mind from going ballistic. It would have been easier to take a pill, but I found that pleading my case before God and allowing the Holy Spirit to strengthen me sustained me. This spiritual life flow is the very thing that the devil wants to suppress in your life. You must do everything you can to keep it flowing. I felt that for me prayer, not pills, would keep the source of life flowing.

We must believe that either the God that we serve can keep and sustain us, or we need to sell out to the world and its dictates. A deadly combination of the two will never work. God wants to keep us at a place where we can pray our way through things, not sit as a zombie under the influence of something that renders us ineffective to fight the good fight of faith.

If the enemy is going to have any influence or control over you he must first *DEPRESS* the Holy Spirit's ability to transmit the life of God to you. To depress means to cast down or put under. If the presence of the Spirit of God is cast down and put under, we are left with nothing but our own carnal thinking to guide us.

Looking at sickness from the perspective of doctor's reports and physical feelings is usually beyond the natural mind's ability to overcome. Taking the available data about your sickness and analyzing it from every possible perspective, the natural mind becomes overloaded dealing with all the multiplied possibilities and will usually resort to the negative. You begin to think about the negative and dwell on the negative, and finally, you become negative.

The scriptures tell us that as a man thinks in his spirit so he becomes (see Proverbs 23:7). Your life is a mirror of your thinking. If it is under the influence of the natural mind, your spirit, which is your connection to God, is buried under the power of negative thinking. Your natural mind is shouting at you louder than the gentle promptings of the Spirit. The more negative your thinking becomes, the more depressed the spirit becomes. Instead of being governed by the mind of Christ, you will be governed by human reason, which has no real or lasting solutions.

One of my favorite stories in the Bible is the account of David and his near disaster in the city of Ziklag (1 Samuel 30). David, who has been anointed King of Israel, is biding his time until God's dealings with Israel and King Saul are completed. David is very much in the will of God and undergoing a preparation that will culminate with his leading the nation of Israel into the most glorious time that the nation will ever enjoy.

Upon returning to their hideaway in Ziklag, David and his men discover that their enemies have ravaged the city, burned their dwellings, stolen their possessions, and kidnapped their families. The men are distraught and completely overwhelmed by what their natural understanding is telling them. They are so angry that they look to David and blame him for the whole mess. They begin to plot among themselves to stone David and secure new leadership.

David, however, does a remarkable thing. He removes himself from the chaos and seeks the face of God. The Bible says that he encouraged himself in God. As he communed with God, he was given supernatural revelation as to what he should do and what the outcome of his obedience would be. God told David to pursue his enemies and that he would recover all that was lost. David did as God commanded and everything that God had spoken to him became a reality.

In times of sickness, we must constantly encourage ourselves in God. In the darkest of circumstances, when in the natural understanding everything seems lost, God can give us a sense of direction that will bring into existence the very thing that our natural mind tells us can never happen. It is imperative that you never allow depression to take root in your life. Your life-giving source, the Holy Spirit, must have the liberty to communicate to your mind what truth is. Romans 12 tells us that we are not to be conformed to this world, but rather be transformed by the renewing of our mind. In other words, the only transformation you can experience is when your mind, with it's natural reasoning, is renewed and under the dominion of the Holy Spirit. Your outlook will change, your countenance will be different, and your faith will sustain you during your toughest battles.

During times of sickness, we must learn to play the hand we have been dealt. There are certain realities that you must deal with and wishing they would go away is not a realistic option. Resenting your situation will rob you of day-to-day little things that make up your life. Resentment will steal from your relationships with family and friends, which leaves you with only your carnal mind dwelling on how unfair your circumstances are.

If you are going to overcome the death grip that sickness wants to ensnare you, you must come to the conclusion that there are certain realities that you must deal with and not allow yourself to drift off into some mental nirvana that just wishes it would all go away. You must survey the situation and devise a battle plan. You must understand that depression is an enemy of wholeness. Recognize the avenue that leads to depression and take whatever detours are necessary to avoid it.

Another death grip sickness brings is *OBSESSION*. It is easy to become obsessed with your dilemma and shut down all other aspects of life and concentrate exclusively on your own needs, but life is in giving. If you shut down your giving, you will cut off the flow of life to yourself. Even when you are sick, life goes on. As much as you possibly can, determine to be a giver. Giving will take your mind off yourself and its needs and will bring a degree of joy to your life as you bless others in your own time of battle.

Being obsessed with yourself shuts you off from everyone and everything around you. If you focus on yourself, your resources consist of only what your strength can bring to the situation. If you choose to give, you will find that God will give back to you in direct proportion to the measure of giving you give to others.

Life flows back to you as you give to others. Never get to the point that the world revolves around you and your sickness. Determine to bless others when you are around them. Always give them more than they give to you. Obsession with sickness will choke out many avenues of blessings that God wants to send your way.

An *OPPRESSOR* is one who rules by putting down all opposition by force. An oppressor wants to remove anything other than himself as the channel of life. Freedom to hear from any other source, freedom to express any other thoughts, and freedom to move from venue to venue for life sustaining power are denied. Only what the oppressor wants you to hear, to feel, and to experience are allowed. The enemy wants to oppress you to the degree that he controls what you think, what you listen to, and what you see. He wants to oppress all sources of life to you. He wants to flood you with lies and bury your spirit under a layer of unholy silt that renders you unable to hear from God.

Never allow the enemy any place in your life. You cannot allow anger, or resentment or a *Why me?* attitude to get a foothold in your life. These attitudes become landing strips for the devil to launch his attacks on your mind. The enemy will use these tactics to oppress everything that will bring you encouragement and help. Constantly be on the alert for anything that wants to reduce your focus and sphere of influence. Keep your channels open and God will sustain you during any battle.

CHAPTER 6

There is Hope Again

I entered IUPUI Medical Center in early April of 1996 full of apprehension and a gnawing sense of dread to take my first chemo treatment. Over and over again I thought, *What will it feel like when this stuff enters my body? Will it hurt? Will I become instantly nauseated? When will my hair fall out? Will I lose feeling in my feet?*

None of these concerns were alleviated when the nurses came in to start the IV. There is no way to put into words the feelings that flood you when you take your first chemo treatment. Wearing protective gloves, the nurses carried the drugs into the room. On the container was the same *DANGER HAZARDOUS MATERIAL* warning you see on semi-trucks carrying hazardous materials down the interstate. *Whoa, I thought, if the nurses are this concerned about getting a drop of this stuff on them, what is a whole bag of it going to do to my insides?* Seeing a container with a blue label with skull and cross bones did not increase my comfort level about what was getting ready to flow into my bloodstream.

When the IV drip started, I kept waiting for the effects to hit me with some sort of powerful force. I waited, and waited, and waited yet nothing negative happened. After the first hour of receiving treatment and being able to endure it, I breathed a sigh of relief. I learned on that first day of treatment, the best way to get through it is to relax, take a nap and sleep through as much of it as you possibly can, and not allowing fear and agitating thoughts to steal your strength and clutter your mind.

At the end of the first week of treatment, I developed flu-like symptoms that intensified after every session. I was nauseated, had no desire to eat, ached in all my joints, and had numbness in both feet. My strength slowly depleted to do simple tasks, like mowing the yard or pushing the grocery cart through Wal-Mart. I found if I over extended myself, my body did not have the ability to bounce back. Strength became precious and had to be rationed at the proper times. I had to find the stamina to minister. I stole strength from other less worthwhile activities and saved it for those times that were the most important to me, Sundays and Wednesdays.

Though I have been afflicted since my early twenties with male pattern baldness, I am very attached to what hair I have. Most of my adult years I have worn a full beard. The day your hair falls out, as any chemo patient will tell you, initiates you into a club you never wanted to join, *The Club of the Seriously Sick*. After the hair loss, it is hard to hide your condition from all the casual observers you encounter in daily life. As you walk in any shopping area, you feel like a billboard that everyone is reading. The disease that is hidden inside you, is now on display for everyone to observe and make mental judgements.

It happened so fast. On Monday there was not even a hint of what was about to happen, but on Tuesday, it was like a switch was flipped and my hair just let loose.

As I removed my hand after scratching my beard, I discovered to my horror, that it was full of hair. I took my hand and dusted my beard right off my face. I rubbed my fingers through my head and they too became covered with hair.

I had dreaded this experience since the first day of chemo. But hair loss is just one of the many humbling experiences that a bout with cancer brings. Wanting to end the process as rapidly as I could, I called my barber, drove the twenty miles to his shop, and yielded to his shears.

My physical appearance was so drastically altered that many of my friends and acquaintances no longer recognized me. I had trouble dealing with the new persona the mirror was reflecting. Many of the distinguishing features that make me the unique character I am, such as hair, beard, eyebrows, and eyelashes had vanished. Replacing my normal reflection was a bizarre hybrid of Mr. Clean and Uncle Fester. The new guy in the mirror took some time to adjust to.

The first Sunday morning service after the hair loss was particularly difficult. Still struggling with my new looks, I hid behind the piano and directed the worship leader to conduct the service until time for me to deliver the morning message. Several members of our congregation seeing the shiny domed preacher sitting in my place assumed I was gone and he was a guest speaker. When my distinct voice revealed the identity of their supposed guest speaker, several people literally jumped in their seats. Though it was somewhat amusing, I had a tough time getting past the looks on people's faces as I delivered the morning message.

The physical effects of chemotherapy humble the patient and serves as a constant reminder of the disease residing within them. I would be pushing a cart through

Wal-Mart mulling over the grocery list, when a stare from a child, observing my pale and hairless features, jolted me back to the reality that I had cancer. My collection of baseball hats became prized possessions. I would not leave the house without a hat, and if my wife had not put up such a squawk, I would have preached on Sunday morning wearing a hat to match my jogging suit.

The resiliency of the human spirit can triumph over all the adversity and side effects of the standard cancer fighting treatment. You learn to adapt to the new image in the mirror, and you return a smile when encountered with a stare. You go on the offensive during conversations with people who want to know but are afraid to ask. You learn to adapt to the physical weakness you experience and conserve energy for the things that are worthwhile. I love golf and was determined that the effects of chemo were not going to rob me of one of the things I enjoy most. I would go to the course, play as many holes as my strength would allow, return home and rest. I love to preach. I would go to church, give the congregation everything I had, and go home and rest.

Chemotherapy taught me to conserve strength and only use my resources for worth while things. One of the biggest problems I see in the church today is that God's people expend all their resources, both natural and spiritual on things that in the scope of eternity matter little. The Apostle Paul, writing to the church at Ephesus tells us not to be drunk with wine, which is dissipation, but be filled with the Spirit (see Ephesians 5:18).

Many well-meaning believers spend all their strength on worldly endeavors and have very little to give to God. They are too tired to pray, read the word, and go to church. They are unable to deposit anything godly into the lives of those seeking God because they have become spiritually bankrupt. I learned a powerful principle during chemo that has become a cornerstone of my existence. You must conserve your energy, emotionally, physically, and spiritually for those things that matter the most.

There are Some Things You Just Cannot Explain

I was convinced that the chemo was not going to have any impact on the tumors in my bladder and felt very strongly that the upcoming reevaluation would confirm my diagnosis. I had yielded to the pleas of friends and family, taken the two treatments, and was now prepared to hear Dr. Rowland compassionately tell me that we had fought a valiant fight, but my medical options were over. At least it was comforting to think that there would be no more hospitals, chemo needles, and hospital food. I was either going to get a miracle or die.

When you have been diagnosed with a potentially deadly condition, you build a wall around your emotions to insulate you from the detrimental effects of bad news. You learn to hear the negative reports but not to allow them to bring your emotions to the surface. The initial negative diagnosis literally flattens you. It is bigger than your ability to deal with it and produces a storm of emotions that tosses you helplessly through the wind it created in your soul. Stunned with the reality of that initial experience, you determine to never allow yourself to get caught in another emotional firestorm so you build a wall around your emotions to contain them. You become determined to look adversity in the eye and not blink.

Our drive to Indianapolis that June morning was devoid of conversation and emotional exchanges. I was going to endure the cystoscope, hear the bad news, thank the medical staff for their efforts, and bid a fond farewell to IUPUI. Nothing anyone could say or do was going to get me emotionally involved.

Because of the location of my tumors, I had become all too familiar with having a cystoscope inserted in my urinary tract. It is a humbling experience to lie unclad on a gurney, while someone I hardly knew examined my most private areas. The procedure lasts between 3-5 minutes. I learned to relax, to cooperate with the physician, and to force my mind to dwell on a more pleasant topic.

After a few pleasantries, I hopped on the table, adjusted my thinking, and waited for the local anaesthetic to kick in. *In three minutes, it will be over with, I thought, and I would never have to do this again.*

As the procedure started, I awaited the usual small talk the doctor used to divert my attention away from the discomfort the cystoscope produces. I could sense an intensity of examination that superceded his prior look to determine the size of the tumors. His silence confirmed my suspicions that the chemo had failed, the tumors had grown, and my prognosis was headed further south.

The words that came from behind the sheet that separated visual contact will forever be etched in my memory. "You have had a remarkable response to the chemo, a dramatic, near miracle-type of reaction to the regiment of drugs you have taken," the doctor cheerfully reported. "The tumors are completely gone and I cannot even find any evidence of where they were." But the same wall I had built around my emotions to keep the negative ones from overflowing kept the positive ones in check as well.

While the urologist was slapping me on the shoulder about my good fortune, congratulating me like someone who had just hit the game winning home run in the seventh game of the World Series, I lay emotionless, unable to respond to the greatest medical report of my life.

While I lay in stunned silence for what seemed an eternity trying desperately to muster up enough faith to believe that I was actually in the realm of reality, a flurry of activity electrified the atmosphere in the examining room. The oncologist had arrived, carrying with him results of prior examinations and was busily comparing them with the test I had just under gone. As I strained to hear their medical chitchat and get a layman's grasp on their terminology, one word kept coming out that I didn't need a medical dictionary to understand *"cure."*

After their mini-medical conference, both doctors sat down beside me and explained that the three golf ball-sized tumors in my bladder were no longer there. In their medical opinion, I had had a dramatic response to the two sessions of chemotherapy or in baseball terms *I had hit a grand slam on a 0-2 count with 2 outs in the bottom of the ninth.*

As I listened to the doctors talking, the words, "remarkable," "dramatic," "near miracle," kept coming up, as well as the word "cure." Both doctors wanted me to take the last four chemotherapy treatments, have another evaluation in three months and if everything remained the same, to have the originally scheduled surgery. Both doctors seemed delighted to tell me that my odds had greatly improved and there was now a strong possibility of a cure.

As I left the examining room to relay the news to Ronda, a spring of pent-up emotions began to seep through the wall I had built to protect myself from all the bad medical news of the past five months. But I simply could not express with proper emotions, the way I was feeling inside. I delivered the best news Ronda had heard in the past months with the countenance of a man about to plan his funeral.

I wanted to shout out the good news, but my body would not let me. It would literally be days before my physical countenance would be able to express the joy that was rising up from my spirit. Ronda, absolutely caught off guard by the wonderful news, burst into tears and danced a little jig in the waiting room rejoicing in the miracle that God had dropped in our laps.

Our conversation on the way home included a topic we had not been able to talk about, the future. Even though that day had brought us new hope, there were still the four treatments of chemotherapy, a major surgery, and extended hospital stay and recovery ahead of us.

If there was one thing this ordeal had taught us, it was to live one day at a time. I knew that the doctors were giving credit to the chemotherapy, but on the drive to Laconia that day, I felt an absolute assurance that God Almighty had touched me in a powerful way and that He had a plan for my future. The prayers of the saints and the power of faith had prevailed mightily against the cancer that was trying to take my life. In the coming months, it would be confirmed to me in a stunning revelation of what percentage medicine had played in my actual recovery.

CHAPTER 7

Finding a Relationship with God in the Midst of Your Problem

There is a strong possibility that the reason you are reading this book is because you are struggling with a physical infirmity. You may have just been diagnosed and are looking for a game plan to counterattack what is coming at you, or you may be in the last stages of cancer and desperately need a miracle. You may be person of great faith or someone who is reading this book because a well-meaning friend or relative thrust it in your lap. The reasons you are reading this story could be any one of a hundred reasons, but there is a good chance that you find yourself in the middle of something that you cannot wish away, pray away, rebuke away, or cast away. Up to this point, it just will not go away so you have to deal with it.

God is not the author of sickness. It is the devil that has come to kill, steal, and destroy. Jesus became flesh to destroy the works of the devil. Every evil thing on this planet, whether it is sickness, hurricanes, tornadoes, or any other natural disaster, is a result of Adam's sin and his forfeiture of dominion to satan. Satan is the god of this natural world for a season, but God has empowered us through His spirit to overcome this world, our sinful flesh, and the devil. We must understand James' admonition in the Bible to "submit yourself to God, resist the devil, and he will flee from you." (see James 4:7) God is not the creator of your problem, nor did He have any hand in causing it. In fact, just the opposite is true; He desperately wants to help you overcome it.

If you have never had a born-again experience that comes through faith in God's grace, your spiritual condition is far worse than any disease you may be battling. You must understand that our physical condition is only temporary, but our spiritual condition is eternal. The born-again believer is assured that though the outer man is progressively decaying and wasting away, his inner self is being progressively renewed day after day (2 Corinthians 4:16). The very Spirit that raised Jesus from the dead dwells in the life of a believer and He has the power to give that same kind of spiritual life to his mortal body (see Romans 8:11).

It is really easy when you desperately need a miracle to go after the hand of God instead of His face. You have a life-threatening dilemma and you want God to take care of it. You may have scanned the bookshelves and airwaves trying to find the "How to" word on how to get God to move on your behalf, but you may have not realized that God is a God of relationship, not programs. If you are outside Christ and after a miracle, file this in your memory bank. If somehow you escape death this time, you are only prolonging the inevitable. "It is appointed for all to die once and then comes the judgement." (Hebrews 9:27) If you are lost you need more than a miracle *you need salvation.*

All of us must "seek first God's kingdom and His righteousness and then everything else will be supplied to us." (Matthew 6:33) All of us must have a residence change from the domain of darkness to the kingdom of His marvelous light.

Everyone on this planet needs a savior and genuine salvation cannot be attained by any other means except through Jesus. Many people feel that they are people of faith, but the object of their faith is not what Jesus did for them, the object of their faith is in their own ability to be good. The Bible explicitly informs us that "the path to eternal destruction is broad and many are on it, but the path to heaven is narrow and few are on it." (Matthew 7:13-14) Contrary to this scriptural fact, the vast majority of Americans, according to Gallop polls, believe they are going to heaven. Why the contradiction?

Most people in America feel that though they may have a few flaws, they are basically pretty good people. Many believe that one day, they will stand before God and watch as the angels place all their good deeds on one side of the scales and all their bad deeds on the other side of the scales. They feel pretty confident that the good they do will outweigh the bad and their entrance to Heaven will be a lock. They look around at all their friends, compare themselves to them, and come out looking all right. Many in America do not feel the need for a savior because they are confident that their goodness will get them into Heaven.

The Law of God is a reflection of His nature. It reveals to man what God expects man to be. But the Law of God has one serious flaw, however, our ability to live it. Many erroneously think God gave us the law to guide us along the way; obeying it the best we can, living it by our own strength, and then having a whimsical Heavenly Father allowing us into Heaven because we put in a good effort.

Romans 3:19-24 gives us the following description of our relationship to the Law:

> *Now we know that whatever the Law says, it speaks to those who are under the Law, so that the murmurs and excuses of every mouth may be hushed and all the world may be held accountable to God. For no person will be justified (made righteous, acquitted, and judged acceptable) in His sight by observing the works prescribed by the Law. For (the real function of) the Law is to make men recognize and be conscious of sin (not mere perception, but an acquaintance with sin which works toward repentance, faith and holy character) But now the righteousness of God has been revealed independently and altogether apart from the Law, although actually it is attested by the Law and the Prophets. Namely, the righteousness of God which comes by believing with personal trust and confident reliance on Jesus Christ (the Messiah) (And it is meant) for all who believe. For there is no distinction. Since all have sinned and are falling short of the honor and glory which God bestows and receives. All are justified and made upright and in right standing with God, freely and gratuitously by His grace (His unmerited favor and mercy) through the redemption which is (provided) in Christ Jesus.*

Every living being on this planet shares this common trait, an inability to measure up to the standards of God. The law was given to us to drive home that very point. My sin, your sin, anybody's sin does one thing, separate us from God. We cannot be reconciled to God by our misguided attempts to placate God through our own efforts to be as good as possible. God's word stands firm, if I violate one ordinance, I have violated the entire code. One sin separates me from God.

You and I must see ourselves as a violator of the Law of God and in desperate need of a savior, or someone who could do something for us that we cannot do ourselves. That someone, that savior is Jesus. Jesus left the portals of glory, donned an earth suit, and through His relationship with the Father came to earth and lived a sinless life on my behalf, because I could not do it.

Everything Jesus did on the earth, He did on my behalf. He overcame sin through His connection to His Father's empowering ability while being fully human. Though He was tempted as we are today, He never yielded to its pull. He overcame the god of this world, His humanity and the positions of fame that many wanted to bestow upon Him. He came with a purpose and nothing could stop Him because the motivation that drove Him was His great concern for our condition *separation from God because of our inability to keep the Law of God*.

Not only did Jesus do some things for us that we could not do, but He also made himself responsible for our sinful condition and reversed our spiritual condition through His death, burial, and resurrection. 2 Corinthians 5:19 tells us that "it was God (personally present) in Christ, reconciling and restoring the world to favor with Himself, not counting up and holding against (men) their trespasses (but canceling them) and committing to us the message of reconciliation (of restoration of favor)."

The God of this universe loves us to the degree that He made himself responsible for our spiritual condition in Adam and He reversed it in Christ. The simple point I am making is that "we all have sinned and fallen short of the glory of God" (see Romans 3:23) and that sin has separated us from God. God gave man the law to reveal to him his condition. Each of us must see that in our present condition, we cannot keep God's Holy Law. The soul that sins shall die according to the Bible and that leaves each of us in a spiritual quandary, desiring favor with God, but unable to attain it through our goodness. The law was given to hush our mouth concerning our goodness and lead us to the only, good, and true one, Jesus. What you and I will never be able to do because of the weakness of our flesh *Jesus did.* Jesus kept the Law of God perfectly and He did it not to impress God, but He did it on my behalf because I could not do it.

Jesus' mission did not end after He had lived a sinless life, but He took that sinless life to a cross and became sin on my behalf. 2 Corinthians 5:21 explains it this way, "for our sake He made Christ (virtually) to be sin who knew no sin, so that in and through Him we might become (endued with, viewed as being in, and examples of) the righteousness of God (what we ought to be, approved and acceptable and in right relationship with Him, by His goodness).

Jesus took upon himself my sin and made himself responsible for what I had done wrong. He became my sin and died because of my inability to keep the Law of God. My inability put Him on the cross and His love for me kept Him there. His death 2000 years ago was really my death. He took upon himself my spiritual condition and died with it. The Apostle Paul, writing to the Colossians, gives us this powerful revelation,

> *And although you at one time were estranged and alienated from Him and were of hostile mind in your wicked activities; Yet now has (Christ, the Messiah)*

reconciled (you to God) in the body of His flesh through death, in order to present you holy and faultless and irreproachable in His (the Father's) presence." He continues by saying, "And you who were dead in trespasses and in the uncircumcision of your own flesh (your sensuality, your sinful carnal nature) (God) brought to life together with (Christ) having freely forgiven us all our transgression, having cancelled and blotted and wiped away the handwriting of the note (bond) with its legal decrees and demands which was in force and stood against us (hostile to us). This (note with its regulations, decrees, and demands) He set aside and cleared completely out of our way by nailing it to (His) cross. (Colossians 2:13-14)

Jesus' death completely satisfies the legal system of God. Jesus died on my behalf. The punishment that I deserved because of my sin, Jesus took upon himself. Isaiah, the Old Testament prophet hundreds of years before Jesus' birth, prophesied what Jesus would one day do for every living man, woman, and child. Isaiah proclaimed,

Surely, He has born our griefs (sicknesses, weaknesses, and distresses) and carried our sorrows and pains (of punishment), yet we (ignorantly) Considered Him stricken, smitten, and afflicted by God (as if with leprosy). But He was wounded for our transgressions, He was bruised for our iniquities; the chastisement (needful to obtain peace and well-being for us was upon Him, and with the stripes (that wounded) Him we are healed and made whole. All we like sheep have gone astray, we have turned every one to his own way; and the Lord has made to light upon Him the guilt and iniquity of us all. (Isaiah 53:4-6)

Although it is a spiritual and historical fact that Jesus died, He did not stay dead very long. Once the regulations and requirements under the legal system of God had been satisfied, Jesus had the very first born-again experience. Jesus, dead with my death, having become the propitiation for my sin, or that which appeased God, was raised from the dead by the power of Almighty God. His resurrection actually was my resurrection as well. He was the first person to die and yet not be overcome by death. God raised Him from the dead on my behalf. Jesus was the first born of many brethren (see Hebrews 2:11). His born-again experience would be the first of millions that would follow as the Gospel, the good news of Jesus was proclaimed around the world.

The Bible proclaims that the very same Spirit that raised Jesus from the dead lives in the life of the believer and will quicken itself in us and give life to our mortal bodies.

It is the grace and kindness of God that should lead us to repentance and saving faith in Jesus. It is God's great love for us that is displayed in His grace epitomized by the things Jesus did for us. His grace is that part of His nature that allows Him to have quality relationships with broken humanity. Grace is wonderful, but it is only one side of the story. God's grace has been extended to every man, but not every man will cash in on the great benefits of God's plan of salvation of man.

Faith is your grip on God. "Without faith it is impossible to please God" (see Hebrews 11:6). God wants man to believe Him at His word. During His earthly ministry, Jesus constantly emphasized the fact that man must believe. I am not talking about an intellectual acknowledgement that Jesus was the Son of God. The demons believe that and shudder at the thought. I am talking about a faith that will connect you to God. "Faith is the substance of the things you hope for and the evidence of the things you cannot see." (Hebrews 11:1) You must believe for yourself that God actually did all these things on your behalf. You must believe that everything that Jesus did, He did on your behalf. You must believe that He was your substitute. You must believe that He lived a sinless life for you, died your death, was buried with your burial, and was resurrected with your resurrection.

Ephesians 2:8-9 says it this way, "For it is by free grace (God's unmerited favor) that you are saved (delivered from judgement and made partakers of Christ's salvation) through your faith. And this (salvation) is not of yourselves (of your own doing, it came not through your own striving) but it is the gift of God. Not because of works (not the fulfillment of the Law's demands), lest any man should boast. (It is not the result of what anyone can possibly do, so no one can pride himself in it or take glory to himself.)"

None of these marvelous things came as a result of anything you have ever done or ever will do. They come to us because of God's marvelous grace. Your faith in these facts will release to you the marvelous benefits of grace, peace with God, and an eternal salvation that will never fade away.

If your are reading this book and have never established a relationship with God through the atoning work of Jesus, I have good news and glad tidings of great joy for you. Though your outer man might be decaying and battling sickness, the same Spirit that raised Jesus from the dead can come into you, quicken itself in you, and give life to your mortal body. Through your faith in His awesome grace, you can ask the Holy Spirit to come into your life, destroy the old man of sin, and birth a new man full of the presence of God. You can have the same born-again experience that Jesus had when God raised Him from the dead.

Pray this simple prayer with faith and a miracle will transpire. Dear Lord Jesus, I believe and have simple faith that I have sinned and have separated myself from all that you are. I now realize that I need a savior. I need someone to do for me what I cannot do for myself. I believe that you lived a sinless life on my behalf. I believe that You took my sin upon yourself and died my death on the cross of Calvary. I believe you were buried with my burial and were raised with my resurrection. I have faith that if I will believe in my heart and confess, with my mouth, these great provisions of grace that I will be saved. Thank you Jesus for your great love for me. I am now asking for Your Spirit to come and dwell in me and give me life. I, by faith, believe that the same Spirit that raised Jesus from the dead now lives in me. Thank you for you this great salvation that is found only in the name of Jesus.

If you prayed that prayer with faith, you are now a member of the household of God. You have peace with God, as well as, the mind of Christ. Your spiritual condition is much more important than your physical condition. One of the main reasons for this little deviation from my story is that I wanted to tell you that although doctors and the medical field were of some help to me during my ordeal, it was only through my relationship with Jesus that I was able to overcome. And I want every reader of this book to have an opportunity to experience the power of relationship with Jesus that sustained me during my battle with cancer.

CHAPTER 8

Conforming Me to His Image

Despite the disappearance of the tumors in my bladder, both the urologist and the oncologist, insisted that I continue the regiment of prescribed chemotherapy. The idea of enduring four more five-day stays in the hospital and taking drugs that ravaged my body was almost more than I could bear. Even though I could see some light at the end of the tunnel, I desperately wanted that chapter in my life to end as soon as possible.

The biggest motivational ploy the doctors used to get me to continue the treatments was the promised removal of the urostomy urinary diversion system they had constructed to do the work of my ailing bladder. To accommodate the urostomy device, I had to wear pants at least one size too large, suspenders, and oversized shirts. The constant care, restrictions on certain activities, and sleeping problems it caused sometimes drove me past my spiritual parameters into fits of anger accompanied by rivers of tears. There were times that I absolutely despised the restrictions it imposed on my life style and the embarrassment it caused. With the goal of the removal of the urostomy as my motivation, I gave myself over to the chemo treatments.

The doctors were fairly confident that after the chemo treatments, followed by a three month recuperation period, I would be able to have the originally intended surgery and have the urostomy removed. I found myself in a Catch-22 situation. I wanted them to reconnect my now cancer free bladder and go on about business as normal, but in their vast medical experience, my greatest chance of long term survival was to have my bladder removed and replaced with one they would construct from parts of my colon.

My impassioned pleas to have my bladder reconnected did not prevail. It was going to be their way or not at all. The surgeon told me in no uncertain terms that he would not reconnect my bladder and assured me that I would not be able to find a surgeon that would. By this stage of the game, I was ready to do anything to get rid of that appliance stuck to my side.

The rules had been defined and I reluctantly agreed to them. After the chemo regiment ended, I would give my body sometime to renew its strength, undergo surgery to have my bladder removed, as well as the urostomy. I would live out my days with a bladder constructed of a borrowed reflux valve and a three-inch section from both my large and small intestine.

During those last four chemo treatments I learned a great deal about endurance. I was confident that the things I was hoping for would be realized if I could just endure the process. Spiritually, the Word of God tells us that "the one who endures to the end will be saved" (see Matthew 24: 13). Anyone who has ever tried to walk with God knows that our faith is only the substance of the things we hope for. Hope keeps us in the game, while faith brings us the substance or the reality for what we believe.

Many times in our lives we do not want to have to endure *anything*. We fail to see that pressing on in difficult times builds endurance in our lives, for without endurance we cannot possibly finish the purposes God has for our lives. We must know with certainty that God takes no delight in believers who shrink back in difficulty or lie down and quit (see Hebrews 10:34).

I understand fully that the outcome of my faith is the salvation of my soul. And that if I will fully submit myself to the process that God is allowing in my life, I will develop enough endurance to overcome every obstacle that the god of this world can throw at me. So many times we want out of the trial before it has accomplished its purpose. "God does cause all things to work together for good for them that love God and are called according to his purpose" (Romans 8:28).

Trials lose their power over us when we submit to the purposes behind them. Trials test our faith. Scriptures admonish us to rejoice when trials come because they reveal the depth of our spirituality (see James 1:2-4). When we are squeezed during difficult times in our lives, the quality of the fruit that resides within us, either good or bad, is exposed. Trials, in essence, are tests orchestrated by God to reveal to the believer the reality of their spiritual maturity. We never fail God's tests. We simply take them over and over and over or until we finally pass. During the last four chemotherapy treatments, I took the same spiritual test several times.

As I stated earlier, trials lose their power over us when we submit to the purposes behind them. In the early stages of the chemo treatments, I simply wanted it to be over. I was weary of the ordeal, had little desire to learn any new spiritual insights, and was conscious of only my own dilemma. I despised what was happening and literally blind to what was going on around me. Without realizing it, I had become so caught up in my own misery that I was losing compassion for those that were in similar situations. Instead of reaching out to others, I withdrew into a shell on Monday and emerged on Friday in time to go home without doing anything productive for anyone during the week.

Before every chemo treatment, I had to have blood tests to determine if I was strong enough to endure that week's treatment. After the blood was drawn, I was escorted to a waiting room to await the results. Everything I ever wanted to know about what cancer was really like but afraid to ask could have been answered by simply looking at the people sitting around me. There were little hairless children in wheelchairs too young to even comprehend what was happening to them, accompanied by parents desperately trying to keep on their game faces. Pale teenagers wearing various types of caps and scarves in a vain attempt to hide their disease waited patiently hoping to hear even the slightest hint of good news. The elderly, many wearing surgical masks, often in wheelchairs, sat quietly awaiting word if their frail conditions would prohibit them from receiving another life stretching treatment. In that room you could see the beginning stages of cancer all the way to its end results.

To fulfill the commission of Jesus, we have to be touched with the feelings of the infirmities of others. During those visits to that waiting room, I was forced to deal with the reality that for most of my life as a healthy pastor, I had little compassion for the sick. Suddenly, I was a part of that world. Although God is not the author of sickness, He was using the trial I was going through to conform me to His image. He became the faithful High Priest because He experienced the human condition. He is able to sympathize with our weakness and problems because He lived the human experience. When I come into the presence of Jesus, I am coming to someone who understands.

Suddenly, I understood sickness. Suddenly, I understood what it was like to have cancer. Suddenly, I understood the mental, physical, and spiritual battles that cancer patients face. It was no longer theory, but something God had worked out in my life that I was to use for the benefit of those who were going to come behind me fighting the same battle that I was going through.

When I submitted to the trials, I began to receive revelation from the Holy Spirit that changed my life forever. The scriptures counsel us "to submit to God, resist the devil, and he will flee from us." Submission to my trial opened up a door of relationship with God that I had never experienced and literally caused the devil to withdraw from the situation taking along with him all his lies, accusations, and fears. Those last four chemo treatments became a spiritual training ground that has completely altered the way I approach those fighting physical infirmities.

In December 1996, after completing the regiment of chemo and allowing my body three months to regain its strength, I underwent surgery at IUPUI to have my bladder and prostate removed and replaced with a continent urinary diversion device. Dr. Randall Rowland performed the successful surgery and after an 11-day stay in the hospital, I was released to carry on with life.

Over the past five years, I have had regular check-ups and am cancer free. I have continued to pastor Grace Tabernacle and travel extensively around the world. In the past two years, I have traveled to El Salvador, Cuba, and Haiti.

In spite of a slight alteration to my plumbing, I live life to the fullest. Rarely, a week passes that I am not contacted to visit someone who is battling cancer. I go to be an encouragement, born of an experience that was forged on the anvil of adversity. People, many times, just need to see a survivor, someone who has overcome the very battle they are facing. Spiritually, isn't that what Christians are, survivors? Heaven is and will be filled with overcomers. The world needs to see survivors and overcomers because it gives them hope for their situation.

I had the greatest doctors and nurses that anyone could possibly hope for, and I am certain they played a role in my recovery, but I have no doubt that God Almighty played a far greater role in my survival. I was never more assured of this fact when I visited the oncologist's office four years after my chemo treatments. There were 24 people in the chemo study group I had participated in, and I had gotten to know several of them personally.

During the doctor's visit, I asked Dr. Bruce Roth, the oncologist who had supervised our group, how the others were doing. Looking me square in the eye, Dr. Roth informed me that I was the only survivor of the 24. I cannot put into words, the absolute sense of humility and absolute awe that overcame me.

Every day, I stand humbled in the presence of God, thanking Him for this second chance at life. I do not understand all the whys and the wherefores, but I do know that God has delivered me for a purpose, and I want to spend the rest of my days fulfilling it.